Laughter
&
Liberation

Laughter
&
Liberation

Harvey Mindess

With a new introduction by
Arthur Asa Berger

Transaction Publishers
New Brunswick (U.S.A.) and London (U.K.)

First Transaction paperback printing 2011
Copyright © 1971 by Harvey Mindess

This book is printed on acid-free paper that meets the American National Standard for Permanence of Paper for Printed Library Materials.

Library of Congress Catalog Number: 2010031366
ISBN: 978-1-4128-1471-3
Printed in the United States of America

Library of Congress Cataloging-in-Publication Data

Mindess, Harvey, 1928-
    Laughter and liberation / Harvey Mindess.
        p. cm.
    Originally pub.: Nash Publishing, 1971.
    Includes bibliographical references.
    ISBN 978-1-4128-1471-3 (alk. paper)
        1. Laughter. 2. Wit and humor. I. Title.

BF575.L3M54 2010
152.4'3--dc22

2010031366

for my father, who always
enjoyed a good joke

Contents

Section Two

Section Three

Acknowledgments

The author and publishers wish to thank the following people:

Random House, Inc. for permission to quote from *Feiffer's Marriage Manual*, copyright © 1962, 1967 by Jules Feiffer.

Mrs. Helen Thurber for permission to quote from "The Admiral on the Wheel," copyright © 1937 James Thurber. Copyright © 1965 Helen W. Thurber and Rosemary Thurber Sauers. From *Let Your Mind Alone*, published by Harper and Row. Originally printed in *The New Yorker*. From "The Shrike and the Chipmunks," copyright © 1940 James Thurber. Copyright © 1968 Helen Thurber. From *Fables for Our Time*, published by Harper and Row. Originally printed in *The New Yorker*. From "The Secret Life of Walter Mitty," copyright © 1942 James Thurber. Copyright © 1960 Helen

W. Thurber and Rosemary Thurber Sauers. From *My World and Welcome to It,* published by Harcourt Brace Jovanovich. Originally printed in *The New Yorker.*

Schocken Books for permission to quote from *Inside Kasrilevke,* by Sholom Aleichem, copyright © 1948, 1965 by Schocken Books, Inc.

Alfred A. Knopf, Inc., for permission to quote from *The World of Sholom Aleichem,* copyright © 1943 by Maurice Samuel.

Alfred A. Knopf, Inc. for permission to quote from *The Stranger,* by Albert Camus, translated by Stuart Gilbert, copyright © 1946 by Alfred A. Knopf.

Beacon Press, for permission to quote from *Fiction and the Unconscious,* copyright © 1957 by Simon O. Lesser.

McGraw-Hill Book Co., Inc. for permission to quote from *Light Armour,* copyright © 1954 by Richard Armour.

Doubleday and Co., for permission to quote from *Bigger than a Breadbox,* copyright © 1967 by Steve Allen.

Atheneum Publishers, Inc. for permission to quote the story "Jewish Poker" from *Look Back, Mrs. Lot,* by Ephraim Kishon. Copyright © 1960 by Ephraim Kishon. Copyright © 1960 by N. Tvessky Publishing Ltd.

Mrs. Elinor Floum, for permission to use her original humorous material.

The quotations from Finley Peter Dunne appear in *Mr. Dooley at his Best,* published by Charles Scribner's Sons, 1938.

The quotations from Mark Twain appear in *The Adventures of Huckleberry Finn, The Mysterious Stranger,* and "The Five Boons of Life."

The quotation from Max Eastman appears in *Enjoyment*

of Laughter, published by Simon and Schuster, 1936.

The chapter entitled "Laughter and Women's Lib" was aided by a research study conducted in collaboration with Mrs. Myrna Kettler.

In the chapter entitled "The Genesis of Humorous Genius," the biographical information on Sholom Aleichem was culled from his daughter's, Marie Waife-Goldberg's, excellent book, *My Father, Sholom Aleichem*, published by Simon and Schuster; the data on Steve Allen's childhood and early career was found in Steve Allen's autobiography, *Mark It and Strike It*, published by Doubleday and Co.; and the quotations from Richard Armour were kindly supplied by him in personal correspondence with the author.

All the drawings were done by Gabriel Kreiswirth. Mr. Kreiswirth is both an artist and a sculptor. He teaches art at West High School in Torrance, California.

Introduction to the Transaction Edition

Harvey Mindess was trained as a clinical psychologist which explains why his book, *Laughter and Liberation,* focuses on a number of the therapeutic functions of humor. The book also has a lot of really great jokes and other humorous texts in it. Mindess uses them to buttress his argument that humor has the unique power to liberate people from excessive psychological burdens generated by our feelings of inferiority, our need to conform, our domination by logic and reason, our tendency to be too serious, our egotism and a number of other psychological afflictions. I will say more about these matters shortly.

He explains the rationale for his book in his introduction in which he suggests that humor is "indispensible to our welfare." He adds:

> *I intend to unearth the roots of humor. I intend to demonstrate that it is no more (and no less) mysterious a characteristic than intelligence or compassion. I intend to argue that it can be cultivated and to indicate how.... My method will be to describe the inner obstacles which block the unfolding of our humorous potentials and to point out the possibilities of overcoming them.*

Humor, he explains, is not something that some people are born with and others lack; people can develop their sense of humor as they grow up. Humor, for Mindess, shouldn't be equated with telling jokes but should be understood, rather, as a frame of mind that we can develop and refine as we age and recognize the paradoxical nature of human behavior.

Laughter and Liberation is divided into two parts: the first deals with the way laughter frees us from a number of "inner obstacles" and the second deals with the relationship that exists between humor and creativity and with Mindess' theory of humor. One of the

1

reasons that humor helps "liberate" us from our various obsessions is that humor is based, in large part, on surprise. The unexpected resolution of jokes can help us escape from the demands of our superegos and "the chains of our perceptual, conventional, logical, linguistic and moral systems."

One of humor's most important powers, Mindess asserts, is its ability to help us to escape from the bonds of conformity and to violate, at times, the codes that shape our behavior. This involves our placing ourselves in a situation in which we neither discard society's rules nor accede to them in a slavish manner. It is humor that provides a kind of elasticity and support for nonconformist moments in our daily lives. As he explains, "if we acquire...the frame of mind in which humor flourishes—the individual, iconoclastic outlook—we have set ourselves on the a springboard to freedom."

Humor also has the power to help us cope with feelings of inferiority that may afflict us. It does this in two ways: first, it helps degrade those who contribute to our feelings of inferiority and second, it derides the quest for superiority, the notion that "getting ahead" is all-important. He points out that retaliatory wit is an important part of most cultures and provides some jokes to show how downtrodden groups use humor to "strike back at oppressors." He offers a classic Jewish joke to show this process.

> *A little Jew in Hitler's Germany brushes by a Nazi office, knocking him off balance. "Schwein!" roars the Nazi, clicking his heels imperiously. To which the Jew, undaunted, makes a low bow and replies "Cohen. Pleased to meet you.*

Humor has been used by Jews over the centuries to help them deal with their marginality and relative powerlessness. As Mindess explains, "the very fact of making fun of our inferior position raises us above it." He offers several other Jewish jokes and argues that Jewish humor is not masochistic, as some have argued, but life-affirming. Humor, he asserts, helps us recognize the absurdity and gross injustice that exists and, in doing so, makes it possible for us to become free and detached observers of our fate.

Mindess also discusses the technique which involves parodying the mindsets of our oppressors to show how absurd they are. He provides the following joke to demonstrate this matter.

> *A little Negro girl smears her face with cold cream. Running to her mother in the kitchen she exclaims, "Mommy, mommy, look at me!"*

The mother replies with an angry "Get that gunk off your face."
The child scurries to her father but the same interchange occurs. Downcast
and pouting, she returns to the bedroom, muttering "I haven't been white for
more than five minutes and already I hate two niggers."

Our sense of humor, then, reinforces our humanity and our bonds with others; humor allows us to accept our limitations and to accept and to love ourselves, imperfect as we may be.

In his chapter on "Freedom from Morality," Mindess explains how humor helps us devalue certain moral inhibitions in two ways: it enables us to "indulge both our sexual promiscuity and our callous disregard for other people's feelings." These are the two major impulses we try to control, which explain why we enjoy sexual humor and aggressive and scatological humor so much. He offers a number of wonderful jokes on these topics. Let me cite a comic poem from the book:

A young monk who lived in Siberia,
Found life growing drearia and drearia,
So he did to a nun
What he shouldn't have done—
And now she's a Mother Superia.

This text (and others he uses) suggests that the sex drive is like an itch that has to be scratched. Ribald humor, a combination of humor and pornography, asserts that we should take our morals and need for love with a grain of salt. Laughter is not "nice" and doesn't follow the moral strictures of the societies in which it is found. This helps explain why it can be so liberating.

Mindess turns next to the matter of reason and the way humor satisfies our need to escape from the strictures and monotony of being logical all the time and helps us to enjoy momentary pleasures of the absurd. This chapter has a number of nonsense riddles and jokes as well as quotes from *Alice in Wonderland*. Let me cite some examples.

You are old, Father William, the young man said,
And your hair has become very white;
And yet you incessantly stand on your head—
Do you think, at your age, it is right?
In my youth, Father William replied to his son,
I feared it might injure my brain;
But now that I'm perfectly sure I have none
Why, I do it again and again.

Q.   What is black and white and red all over?
A.   A blushing zebra.

"Didn't we meet in Chicago?"
"No, I've never been to Chicago."
"Neither have I. Must have been two other fellows."

What these nonsense texts do, Mindess reminds us, is to help us recognize of that reason is often fallible. Jokes, he adds, that may be devastating to our identities as professionals (say professors) may be liberating to our identities as human beings.

In his chapter on "Freedom from Seriousness," Mindess explains that one of the great virtues of humor is that it enhances our sense of play and enables us to regain the carefree spirit of our childhood. As he writes "The aim of our sense of humor is not to reduce us to a childish state of mind but to enliven our adulthood with injections of our childishness.... Once we have learned how to care, we must remember how not to care."

Thus, our sense of humor cushions us from the burdens and cares of our everyday activities and helps reconcile us to the pains and failures that are part of everyone's lives. Humor then becomes a kind of antidote that helps us maintain our equilibrium.

In the first section of *Laughter and Liberation*, Mindess lists nine different ways in which laughter frees us from various psychological and social burdens. From a Freudian perspective, we can say that all of these freedoms—and I've discussed a number of them in detail—have the function of supporting and empowering our egos, and to some degree the id elements in our psyches, in their endless battles with superego elements in our psyches.

In Freud's structural hypothesis, he deals with the relationship that exists between the id, ego, and superego elements in our psyches. Freud described the id in his *New Introductory Lectures on Psychoanalysis* as follows:

> *We can come nearer to the id with images, and call it a chaos, a cauldron of seething excitement. We suppose that it is somewhere in direct contact with somatic processes, and takes over from them instinctual needs and gives them mental expression, but we cannot say in what substratum this contact is made. These instincts fill it with energy, but it has no organization and no unified will, only an impulse to obtain satisfaction for the instinctual needs in accordance with the pleasure principle.*

Laughter and humor, we can suggest, helps the id in its struggle to obtain pleasure and gratify instinctual needs.

At every step, however, id elements in our psyches must contend with our superegos. One of the best descriptions of the superego is found in Charles Brenner's classic text, *An Elementary Textbook of Psychoanalysis*. Brenner writes (1974:38):

> *The superego corresponds in a general way to what we ordinarily call conscience. It comprises the moral functions of the superego. These functions include (1) the approval or disapproval of actions and wishes on the ground of rectitude, (2) critical self observation, (3) self-punishment, (4) the demand for reparation or repentance of wrongdoing, and (5) self-praise or self-love as a reward for virtuous or desirable thoughts and actions. Contrary to the ordinary meaning of "conscience," we understand that the functions of the superego are often largely or completely unconscious.*

Mediating between these two forces in the human psyche—our id's desire for pleasure and our superego's fear of punishment—is the ego. It functions by storing experiences in our memories, avoiding overly strong stimuli through flight and focusing its attention on the real world.

Hinsie and Campbell describe the ego in their *Psychiatric Dictionary* (4th edition) as follows (1970: 247):

> *In psychoanalytic psychology, the ego is that part of the psychic apparatus which is the mediator between the person and reality. Its prime function is the perception of reality and adaptation to it.... The various tasks of the ego include perception, including self perception and self awareness; motor control (action); adaptation to reality; use of the reality principle.*

What Mindess does, in the first part of the book, is suggest ways in which humor supports the ego and helps enhance positive aspects of id elements in our psyches. Humor helps liberate us as we battle against the extremely powerful forces of the superego. Freud was interested in humor and wrote an important book on humor, *Jokes and Their Relation to the Unconscious* that, like Mindess' book, is full of wonderful jokes (many of them Jewish jokes) and other examples of humor.

After discussing numerous ways in which humor can liberate us, Mindess offers a chapter on ways of developing a sense of humor. We do this, he suggest, by becoming nonconformists and iconoclasts. As he writes, "Aware of our society's, our peers, and our family's expectations, we must not allow ourselves to function as their servants." Here, quite explicitly, he is making an argument for using humor to fight superego elements of conscience, guilt and, associated with them, the expectations which our families and societies put on us. He continues on with this approach later in the chapter:

Born into a family, a community, a culture, endowed with regularly re-curring needs, we cannot help but learn to control ourselves. We are taught to suppress our impulses, to conform to our surroundings, and in so doing we discover that the effort pays dividends. Every sacrifice of our instincts calls forth some reward; every advance in socialization is remunerated by the group.... From the moment we begin to be socialized, we are thrust into paradox, for we are doomed to suffer from the attainment of the very attri-butes we must strive to achieve.

It is human nature, he argues, that evolved humor as an "out," a means of escape, and an antidote to the pressures and the pain we feel as we sacrifice pleasure to conformity and desire to conscience.

In the second section of the book Mindess focuses his attention on topics such as the relation between humor and creativity, the art of telling jokes, the ways we can discover ourselves through laughter, the use of humor in therapy and theories of humor.

He suggests that there is a relationship between our creativity and our sense of humor, since both involve putting ideas together in new and surprising ways. Thus, in his analysis of jokes, which we can define as short narratives with punch lines that create mirthful laugh-ter, he offers a diagram in which the narratives found in jokes have a beginning, a pause, and then instead of moving on to what might seem to be a logical conclusion, are diverted and end up elsewhere. As he writes, "the line of thought appears to be traveling toward one sort of destination, but it ends up hitting another target altogether."

Humor, Mindess argues, involves leading us to a conventional resolution of a train of thought and then surprising us and diverting us to a different train of thought. He offers an example:

"Always be sincere—whether you mean it or not."

It is the second part of this maxim, which is unexpected and in-volves a logical contradiction, which makes it a humorous state-ment. As he explains, "From pure absurdity to pointed barbs, the play of wit puts pieces of thought together to create brand new ideas.... Humor, moreover, is not just a key to creativity, it is, itself, a creative act."

When it comes to telling jokes, the two most important factors to keep in mind, he suggests, involve timing and mimicry or what he calls "caricature." This involves portraying and parodying the different characters involved in a joke. Because of the difficulties involved in telling jokes, few people can tell jokes well.

Since jokes often involve hostility and aggression and many jokes are sexually provocative, the question arises—why do people enjoy listening to jokes? Mindess offers several ideas to explain our joy in humor: we enjoy humor because we can participate in aggression and sexually provocative jokes in a guilt free manner. We get all the pleasure and none of the pain, so to speak. The other factor is that humor functions as an agent of sublimation that redirects our aggression in acceptable ways and reminds us all of our common humanity. He offers two jokes on these matters: the first reflects hostile aggression and the second deals with sexuality.

> *A man and his wife are watching television. There is a knock at the door. The man calls out, "Who's there?" A voice answers "It's the Boston Strangler."*
> *Turning to his wife, the man says "It's for you, dear."*

> *Arriving home unexpectedly, a husband finds his wife in bed with another man. "See here," he shouts, "Just what do you think you're doing?" "You see," says the wife to the man beside her, "Didn't I tell you he was stupid?"*

There are problems, I believe, with focusing on jokes as a means of generating humor. Doing so suggests that telling jokes is the most important way for people to amuse others and be funny. I don't believe this is correct. In my work I have isolated a number of different techniques that can be used to generate mirthful laughter, such as absurdity, allusions, exaggeration, facetiousness, irony, imitation, word play that we can use to facilitate mirthful laughter. Jokes use many of these techniques, but the techniques are effective on their own, without having to be incorporated into jokes. In addition, some people cannot tell jokes very well, some jokes aren't worth telling, and there is always the possibility that people have already heard the joke you tell, which leads to fake laughter on the part of those being told the joke and is socially uncomfortable.

In addition to giving pleasure to others, Mindess argues, our humor, like our dreams, is also an agent of self discovery. He begins his discussion of this topic with a proposition that what we laugh at has both collective and personal significance. Some things are found humorous by almost everyone in a given society, but individuals all have preferences for the kinds of humor they enjoy. He writes, "Some of us clearly enjoy hostile wit more than others; some dwell persistent on off-color stories; some love absurdity or philosophical humor. Our preferences, we may assume, reflect the state of our psychic economy."

Thus, the kind of humor we like can be seen as a signifier of the things that interest us and occupy our minds.

Humor, itself, and our sense of humor, are useful to therapists on a number of ways. As Mindess explains:

> *Catharsis, insight, self-acceptance, reconditioning, and emotional openness: these experiences, by and large, have been the classical agents of psychotherapy. By fostering one or more of them, psychologists and psychiatrists have attempted—and sometimes even managed—to help their patients cope with their distress.*

To his list of therapeutic agents Mindess adds another powerful agent—humor. It is, in its broadest sense, an approach to life and a frame of mind. Humor is characterized by a number of qualities, he writes, such as "flexibility, spontaneity, unconventionality combined with shrewdness, playfulness, and humility." These qualities play a role in creating what we might call a humorous outlook on life.

There is an ongoing debate among therapists about the use of humor in therapeutic sessions. Some therapists don't believe in using humor in therapy because they believe it functions as a diversion or can have a negative impact on patients. Mindess believes that it is acceptable for therapists to use humor, but they must be very guarded in the way they use it. There is a journal, *Humor and Health,* that makes the case that humor should have an important role in therapy. It describes itself as "Dedicated to humor and laughter and communicating their relationship to holistic health with respect to medical, psychological, social, and spiritual well-being." It offers articles on the use of humor in therapy such as "Clinical Diagnosis and Psychotherapeutic Treatment of Burnout Disorder (BD)P in Physicians: An Emotokinetic Approach," by Waleed Anthony Salameh, the editor and publisher of the journal.

Mindess offers a test that he asserts will enable readers to assess their sense of humor. He tells twelve jokes and asks readers to evaluate each joke on a five point scale, from very funny to not funny. Here are the first four jokes and the numbers he assigns them. He uses the term "joke" loosely, meaning humorous text, since not all of the examples he offers are, technically speaking, jokes.

1. Love is a disease that creates its own antibody, marriage.
2. Q. What does a 500-lb canary say?
   A. CHURP!
3. A famous actor is accosted by a whore. He spends the night at her place. When he is leaving she says, "But you didn't give me anything." So he gives her two tickets to a matinee. She objects. "I don't want to see a show. I'm hungry. I need bread." To which he replies, "If you need bread, screw the baker. From me you get tickets to the theatre.
4. "Mama, Mama—daddy's on fire!"
   "Okay, honey—get the marshmallows."

Each of these jokes, he explains, is an example of a different kind of humor and all of his twelve jokes can be places in one of the four categories of humor:

Joke 1: philosophical
Joke 2: nonsensical
Joke 3: sexual
Joke 4: hostile

These categories are important because they form the basis of a theory of humor that Mindess offers us. Just as moths are drawn, irresistibly, towards flames, writers about humor cannot resist dealing with theories of humor—the subject of his Appendix.

He begins his Appendix with a restatement of his thesis—that humor should be seen as an agent of psychological liberation. He adds:

> Since we were able to include every kind of wit and humor under the umbrella of this thesis, it amounts to an informal but comprehensive theory of the ludicrous. Briefly put, the theory proposes that the most fundamental, the most important function of humor is to release us from the many inhibitions and restrictions under which we live out daily lives.

These restrictions, as I pointed out earlier, are functions of our superegos which, for Mindess, tend to dominate the ego and id elements in our psyches. He then compares his liberation thesis with two other "core" theories of humor, which he labels incongruity and degradation theories.

He quotes Kant's statement that laughter is "an affection arising from the sudden transformation of a strained expectation into nothing," which was the basis of the works of many other incongruity theorists such as Schopenhauer. "To state it simply." Mindess writes, "according to this viewpoint laughter is evoked whenever we are led to expect one image or idea and then we are suddenly presented with another." But he argues that in many jokes, whose punch lines lead us in different directions than we expected to go, the punch lines often do not offer examples of incongruity, just surprise. He adds:

> *Not only is the incongruity theory, as we have seen, contradicted by the very material that confirms it, but we must sense that its aim is far too intellectual. It ignores the emotional, gut-level content of humor: the familiar, repeated expressions of lust, hostility, rivalry, or even the more delicate feelings of compassion and tenderness which put meat on the bones of comedy.*

He then moves on to the second theory of humor, which he calls degradation but which is commonly known as the superiority theory of humor.

He offers a version of a famous quote from Hobbes' *Leviathan,* "The passion of laughter is nothing else but sudden glory arising from some sudden conception of eminency in ourselves." This quotation is incomplete and misses an important aspect of Hobbes' thought. To Mindess' version of this quotation we should add what Hobbes wrote, "by comparison with the infirmity of others, or with our own formerly." This addition fleshes out Hobbes' theory and reminds us that humor can be self-reflexive: we can laugh at others but also at ourselves when we were "inferior" to our later stages of development. What we call the superiority theory of humor actually can be found in Aristotle's writings. He argued in his *Poetics* that:

> *Comedy is an imitation of men worse than average; worse, however, not as regards any sort of fault, but only as regards one particular kind: the Ridiculous, which is a species of the ugly. The Ridiculous may be defined as a mistake or deformity not productive of pain or harm to others; the mask, for instance, that excites laughter, is something ugly and distorted without causing pain."*

Comedy developed, Aristotle wrote, as improvisations on phallic songs that evolved into comic revels, which then became dramatic works in which characters acted out the stories.

Mindess doesn't like the superiority theory because it involves "downgrading others and bolstering our self-esteem" and, as such, has negative psychological consequences. Superiority theory also can't deal with nonsense humor. He offers several examples of this humor.

> *Q. What is purple, weighs ten tons, and is found in the ocean?*
> *A. Moby Plum.*
> *Q. How can you tell if there's an elephant in your refrigerator?*
> *A. You'll find his footprints in the cheesecake.*

Where, Mindess asks, do you find superiority? Neither the incongruity theory nor the degradation/superiority theory of humor can fully explain humor, he asserts. Only his liberation theory, he asserts, is adequate to the task:

> *It elucidates the entire, varied range of things that make us laugh, omits neither intellectual, perceptual, nor emotional components, and—most important—makes convincing sense of the fact that wit and comedy are, above all, delightful... With regard to jokes and other forms of wit, it also provides a more comprehensive explanatory system than the other leading theories.*

He explains, later, that the incongruity and degradation/superiority theories can be seen as components of his "liberation" theory.

In making this argument, Mindess is similar to many other writers on humor who write that their favorite theory of humor, whether it is superiority or incongruity, is the only valid theory that explains humor in an adequate and comprehensive manner. What Mindess calls his "liberation" theory may be seen as an amplification of another important theory of humor, Freud's psychoanalytic theory that is found in his classic work *Jokes and Their Relation to the Unconscious*. In the introduction to Freud's book he quotes Jean Paul, who wrote "Freedom produces jokes and jokes produce freedom." That is the argument that Mindess fleshes out in his book. In his chapter on "The Purposes of Jokes," Freud discusses smutty jokes and hostile jokes and writes:

> *A joke will allow us to exploit something ridiculous in our enemy which we could not, on account of obstacles in the way, bring forward openly or consciously; once again, then, the joke will evade restrictions and open sources of pleasure that have become inaccessible.*

Another Freudian, Martin Grotjahn, wrote a book that used Freud's insights into humor to investigate its impact on our lives and suggest its various therapeutic functions—*Beyond Laughter: Humor and the Subconscious*. This book was published in 1966, five years before the Mindess book. Other writers, such as psychiatrist William Fry, have also written extensively on the therapeutic significance of laughter and humor. I have also written on this subject, though my work focuses upon the therapeutic consequences of the techniques of humor.

The great contribution Mindess has made to our understanding of humor is that he has shown how humor can function as a positive force in our mental lives. He has offered us a well written, entertaining, and accessible guidebook about the way humor can help us find a way to balance the repressive superego forces in our psyches with enhanced id and ego functions. Freud, we may say, opened the door to our understanding of the functions of humor in the human psyche.

Mindess concludes his book as follows:

> *It remains to be said, of course, that despite this supporting evidence and all other arguments that might be marshaled to bolster our position, our approach to humor is not by any means the last word on the subject. Nor it is meant to me. Every theory or explanation, as a system of logic and language, is doomed to partial representation of a phenomenon like humor, for in essence the ludicrous spans the boundaries of reason and words as it emerges out of a deeper, prior realm of being.*

Laughter and Liberation is a actually a kind of self-help book, written by a therapist with a wonderful sense of humor, whose purpose is to help his readers find more joy and pleasure in life by showing the incredible power of that fascinating and ineffable phenomenon we know as humor. His book takes its place as an important contribution both to the study of humor and to the practice of psychotherapy.

Arthur Asa Berger, June 2010

Bibliography

Berger, Arthur Asa. (1993). *An Anatomy of Humor.* New Brunswick, NJ: Transaction Publishers.

Brenner, Charles. (1974). An *Elementary Textbook of Psychoanalysis.* Revised Edition. Garden City, NY: Anchor Nooks.

Freud, Sigmund. (1905/1963). *Jokes and Their Relation to the Unconscious.* Transl. James Strachey. New York: W.W. Norton.

Freud, Sigmund. (1933/1965). *New Introductory Lectures on Psychoanalysis.* Transl. James Strachey. New York: W.W. Norton

Fry, William. (2010). *Sweet Madness: A Study of Humor.* New Brunswick, NJ: Transaction Publishers.

Grotjahn, Martin. (1966). Beyond *Laughter: Humor and the Subconscious.* New York: McGraw-Hill.

Hinsie, Leland E. and Robert Jean Campbell. (1970) *Psychiatric Dictionary.* Fourth Edition. New York: Oxford University Press.

Introduction

Our sense of humor is, without a doubt, one of our most valuable faculties. Thinkers simple and profound agree that the ability to see the funny side of things, to savor the ridiculous in life, and to laugh at ourselves and our troubles is an asset of the greatest magnitude. Yet no one seems to know how to *cultivate* their own, or anybody else's, sense of humor. Beyond exhorting each other to "laugh it off," we have little of substance to suggest.

Some writers settle for the notion that a sense of humor is a God-given gift. Either we have it or we don't, they imply, and there they let the matter rest. Others believe we can acquire the faculty simply by deciding to practice it. Resolve to chuckle, they advise, and magically our careworn hearts will be lightened. Their hopes may be sincere, but I doubt that their advice has helped a single suffering soul.

Besides, both views are naive. Our psychological abilities develop gradually, affected by a host of factors, to whatever degree of excellence they attain. Neither our intelligence nor our compassion, for example, is entirely innate; nor can either be turned on by a simple act of will. Our sense of humor is no different. While inborn qualities may predispose it and conscious efforts may facilitate it, in the largest sense it waxes and wanes as part of our psychic economy. It is determined by our other needs and in turn contributes to them.

How this pattern operates is the theme of this book. I intend to unearth the roots of humor. I intend to demonstrate that it is no more (and no less) mysterious a characteristic than intelligence or compassion. I intend to argue that it can be cultivated and to indicate how. Not, however, in the form of easy exercises or sure-fire steps to a life filled with laughter, for that in itself would be a joke. My method will be to describe the inner obstacles which block the unfolding of our humorous potentials and to point out the possibilities of overcoming them.

We tend to believe that laughter and the state of mind associated with it are reactions which other people or events must evoke in us. As a consequence, we allow ourselves to deteriorate into mere recipients of jokes and professional comic routines. I intend to show that all of us can be creators of laughter too, that we can exercise our sense of humor as an active, effective faculty which we can bring to bear on life in all its apects.

But is not this entire enterprise a triviality? In times like the present, when misery and hatred flourish, should we not be occupied with more important topics? To put it bluntly, why bother with humor? Let our answer be equally blunt: because it is indispensible to our welfare. Like love, courage, and understanding, it is one of the attributes that can sustain us through the worst. In its lesser manifestations it can lighten the load of our daily cares; at its peaks it can enable us to live joyous lives in the midst of all our suffering.

A flourishing sense of humor is fundamental to mental health. It represents a source of vitality and a means of transcendence second to none. Fostering its development, however, is not exactly a merry game. It poses a challenge to our dearest conceits and demands the sacrifice of our defenses against insecurity. We can anticipate, therefore, that once we have learned its key most of us will choose to forget it. Let us not complain about it, though, for if we didn't—what would there be to laugh at?

Section
One

From Laughter to Humor

If you tell a joke to a peasant, he will laugh three times: first, when you tell it; second, when you explain it; and third, when he understands it.

If you tell it to a landowner, he will laugh twice: first, when you tell it; and second, when you explain it; for he never understands it.

If you tell it to a Cossack, he will laugh only once: when you tell it; for he does not let you explain it, and that he cannot understand it goes without saying.

If you tell it to another Jew, however, he will not laugh at all. Before you're half-way through he'll stop you, shouting, "That's an old one! I've heard it before, and besides—I can tell it better."

A superb example of Jewish wit, this traditional anecdote has merit on more than one level. Its structure is elegant, its social critique is neat, and, though this is hardly its point, it makes an important observation. People, it reminds us, differ in their sense of humor.

Stated so baldly, the assertion seems banal. No man in his right mind will debate it, nor will many of us give it a second thought. Yet its implications are highly significant. If our sense of humor is, as we know it is, an invaluable capacity, then our ability to exercise it is as crucial to our welfare as our ability to love. And if a fully developed sense of humor is, as I hope to show it is, our ultimate hope in this age of despair, then its cultivation is as important as any other task we can undertake.

Why then do people differ in this faculty? Is it simply, as our anecdote suggests, a matter of stupidity versus intelligence? And what is a fully developed sense of humor anyway? Is it the ability to get the point of jokes, or does it have anything to do with jokes at all?

Despite the astuteness of our illustration, there is more to the matter than it implies. Intelligence can, without question, contribute to humor, but it does not guarantee it. Many a brilliant man suffers from a sad deficiency of wit, while many a stupid one enjoys a lively capacity for laughter. And the appreciation of jokes, or even the ability to tell jokes effectively, is a criterion of humor only in a superficial sense. As the Hollywood sex symbol may, in real life, make a lousy lay, the professional comedian need not by any means command a genuine sense of humor.

Is a fully developed sense of humor, then, the ability to create spontaneous jests, to be personally witty and amusing —or does it extend beyond that too? We will soon come to see that it does. We will come to see that our sense of humor ranges beyond jokes, beyond wit, beyond laughter itself. While we will begin by examining laughter and funny stories, our study will lead us to a realm of experience that has no such tangible representation.

Humor, in the essence we are about to pursue, is a frame of mind, a manner of perceiving and experiencing life. It is a kind of outlook, a peculiar point of view, and one which has great therapeutic power. It can enable us to survive both failure and success, to transcend both reality and fantasy, to thrive on nothing more than the simplicity of being. Our sense of humor, in the deepest sense, is our ability to awaken and maintain this exceptional frame of mind.

Few of us, unfortunately, can lay claim to its fullness. The question is why. Why are we supposedly mature adults seldom able to actualize the possibilities of this faculty? To lay the groundwork for our answer, let us turn back to our beginnings, to the roots of laughter as they exist in infancy. If we understand what humor stems from, we will be in a position to comprehend the conditions that hinder the flowering of its most magnificent blossoms.

Within a few months after birth, all healthy infants laugh easily. Among the earliest laughter-provoking stimuli, two appear to be predominant. They are, first, mother (or any other familiar and comforting person) making an unusual face and, second, parents (or persons the child relies on for security) tossing the baby in the air and catching him in their arms.

What may we infer? Both the face-making and the tossing are disruptions of the infant's cozy life; both are sudden, brief distortions of his usual experience. They upset his stability, jolt him out of his little rut, and he delights in them as long as they are mild enough for him to tolerate. Now the intriguing analogue is this: disruption, distortion, the jolt—the experience of being jerked out of a rut—is an integral aspect of all types of humor.

In jokes, for example, we are led along one line of thought

and then booted out of it. The twist or the punch line does the job; it is the joke's equivalent to the baby's flight or his perception of an unexpected set of facial features.

Three men lay dying on a hospital ward. Their doctor, making rounds, went up to the first and asked him his last wish. The patient was a Catholic. "My last wish," he murmured, "is to see a priest and make confession." The doctor assured him he would arrange it, and moved on. The second patient was a Protestant. When asked his last wish, he replied, "My last wish is to see my family and say goodbye." The doctor promised he would have them brought, and moved on again. The third patient was, of course, a Jew. "And what is your last wish?" the doctor asked. "My last wish," came the feeble, hoarse reply, "is to see another doctor."

Here, as in the vast majority of funny stories, we are led to anticipate one sort of outcome and presented with another. The same holds true of spontaneous witticisms and deep-going humorous insight. Rather than operate in the expected, logical, or proper manner, the humorous mind skips about, shifts its view, and comes up with a surprising observation. "I can safely say I have no prejudices," Mark Twain once declared. "Let a man be black or white, Christian, Jew, or Moslem—it's all the same to me. All I have to know is that he's a human being. He couldn't be worse."

From Twain to Thurber to Feiffer to Perelman, from Laurel and Hardy to "Laugh-In," the comic spirit is an embodiment of the spirit of disruption. It breaks us free from the ruts of our minds, inviting us to enjoy the exhilaration of escape.

The stimuli which rouse our laughter in infancy disrupt our perceptual system, the system through which we first organize our raw experience. When the baby sees his mother's face distorted or feels himself flying through the air, he discovers the glee of being freed from the very source of his security. As we become acculturated, however, we acquire other organizing systems as well. Conventions, logic, language, morals: all are arrangements for structuring our raw experience, for bringing sense and order into our lives. Like the baby's crib and mother, they are crucial to our security. They are also, however, deadening to the flow of sensation, impulse, thought, and feeling which arises out of our natural vitality.

When, in the interests of good citizenship, we restrain our desires to steal, cheat, lie, swear, gluttonize, fornicate, attack, and destroy; when, in the interests of sanity, we banish strange fantasies and irrational ideas from our minds; when, in the interests of adjustment, we abide by the habits and fashions of our society, we achieve a mixed blessing. On the one hand, we amass security and peace of mind; on the other, we sacrifice spontaneity and genuineness.

Here, then, is the essential irony of our human condition: the very acquisitions that provide our stability split us off from our authentic selves. And that—precisely—is where humor comes in. In the most fundamental sense, it offers us release from our stabilizing systems, escape from our self-imposed prisons. Every instance of laughter is an instance of liberation from our controls.

A lively sense of humor requires first a readiness to slip loose from organized modes of being. To enjoy it, we must be able to delight in disinhibition, to revel in utter foolishness. We must be willing to be impulsive, irreverent, impertinent. We must be capable of being unashamedly childish.

All humor is built on this foundation, but once we have reached maturity the foundation alone is not enough. Once we have been robbed of innocence, we are compelled to develop another dimension as well. We are compelled to understand: to understand human nature and human destiny, not in a theoretical or scientific fashion, but in a shrewd, sagacious way. Once we have known betrayal, corruption, defeat, no reversion to childish bliss is viable. Laughter grows out of a pristine state of fluidity, but to burgeon into full-flowered humor it must be fed with an awareness of the eternal human comedy.

A wit declares, "I used to be an atheist, but I gave it up. No holidays." We may appreciate the jest at various levels. It is funny as a frivolous remark and as a put-down of the seriousness with which people take their religious affiliations. Beyond that, however, it contains a nugget of truth: the truth that our lofty religious and philosophical convictions really serve very mundane needs. The man who enjoys it at that level can be said to possess a more fully developed sense of humor than the man who does not.

But jokes and quips, as we have already noted, fail to plumb the depths of humor. The material on which it flourishes is far more natural. Listen, sometime, to an ordinary conversation between two old friends:

> *"Hi there. How are you?"*
> *"Fine thanks. How's yourself?"*
> *"Not bad. What ya been up to?"*
> *"Nothing much. How about you?"*
> *"About the same. Let's get together sometime."*
> *"Right. Let's get together."*
> *"I'll be seein' you"*
> *"Be seein' you."*
> *"So long."*
> *"So long."*

The insipid dialogue is worldwide; we are all participants in its counterparts every day of our lives; and since what we claim we crave is real relationship—a sense of communication, of knowing and touching and caring for each other—the situation is not devoid of irony. Could we tune in to the speakers' thoughts, moreover, the irony would be compounded. It is probably no exaggeration to imagine they might run like this:

A rash of ironies, in fact, severely freckles the face of our existence. From the circumstance that those we love we often hate while those we hate we often envy, to the certainty that whatever we strive for is anticlimactic when we obtain it, a plethora of incongruities embroiders our lives. Nothing is exactly as it seems or nearly as we claim: that is the earth out of which sophisticated humor grows.

In order to command an adult sense of humor, then, we must keep ourselves aware of the paradoxes that characterize human behavior. We must know, not just in our heads but in our bones, that persons who preach altruism are motivated by egotism, that assertiveness is the mask of fearfulness, that humility is a kind of pride, that love is a euphemism for lust, that truth is the pawn of fashion, that we cherish our misery, and that we are all more irrational than we acknowledge.

We must know these things not as abstract principles but as practical rules of thumb. While our reason and idealism may be confounded at what goes on in the world, our deeper comprehension must expect it and enjoy it. If we are loyal, devoted spouses, we must understand that naturally we crave promiscuous liaisons. If we take a mistress or a lover to make up for what our marriage lacks, we must not be surprised to find that, instead of one problem, we now have two. If we are dreamers who laud the self-indulgent life, we must suspect that we really wish we could buckle down to hard work. Should we begin to work, however, we must anticipate that we will soon miss the lazy life we left behind.

A cartoon strip by Jules Feiffer expresses this outlook succinctly. It shows a housewife musing, "By the time George told me he was leaving on a business trip for a month I had lost all feeling for him. . . . Each dinner when he'd come home I'd try to rekindle the flame, but all I could think of as he gobbled up my chicken was: 'All I am is a servant to you, George. . . .' So when he announced he had to go away I was delighted. While George was away I could find myself again! I could make plans! . . . The first week George was away I went out seven times. The telephone never stopped ringing. I had a marvelous time! . . . The second week George was away I got tired of the same old faces, same old lines. I remembered what drove me to marry George in the first place. . . . The third week George was away I felt closer to him than I had in years. I stayed home, read Jane Austen and slept on George's side of the bed. . . . The fourth week George was away, I fell madly in love with him. I hated myself for my withdrawal, for my failure of him. . . . The fifth week George came home. The minute he walked in and said, 'I'm back, darling!' I withdrew. . . . I can hardly wait for his next business trip so I can love George again."

In its early stages, our sense of humor frees us from the chains of our perceptual, conventional, logical, linguistic, and moral systems. The unexpected act, the startling remark, the nonsense quip, the pun, and the dirty joke are all, in the beginning, parties to our conspiracy of escape. In its more sophisticated stages, it releases us from our naive belief that man is a reasonable, trustworthy creature. Disillusioning wit joins the company of our abettors. To attain its ultimate, however, it must liberate us from identification with our own egos, for in this feat resides its quintessential power.

Tom Lehrer, the gifted comic singer, spoofs himself with versatility. On the jacket of an album entitled *An Evening (wasted) with Tom Lehrer*, we may read: "This recording was made in Tom Lehrer's living room one evening when a few friends had dropped in and conversation was becoming strained. In a desperate attempt to save the evening . . . Mr. Lehrer rushed to the piano and performed the program heard here, making up the songs as he went along. Thanks to a quick-thinking engineer, who had happened by with his pockets full of recording tape, the whole fiasco has been preserved for posterity. . . . In the hope of making the record slightly less wearisome, a certain number of coughs, hisses, snores, impacts, etc., have been edited out. . . . If, despite these deletions, the record is still too tedious for you, you may wish to follow the procedure adopted by many owners of Mr. Lehrer's LPs and play it at 78 rpm, so that it is over with that much sooner."

Lehrer, of course, is posturing for an audience, so his self-mockery may be no more than a ploy to gain applause. In like manner, all of us make fun of ourselves at times to impress others with our apparent modesty or to ward off satirical attacks from outside. When, however, in a reflective moment, we really see how silly our ambitions and regrets, achievements and failures are, we inhale the rarefied atmosphere of selflessness—and that, if anything, is humor's crowning gift.

A patient of mine once tossed off the remark, "My problem's simple. I'm a total mess." Coming as it did on the heels of her tale of woe, it broke us both up. We laughed in mutual delight, and the patient's ability to weather her storms seemed resuscitated.

How did her observation help? In a number of ways, I would say. First, by exaggerating her plight she reduced the significance of her actual problems. In comparison to a total mess, a partial mess is not so bad. Second, by proclaiming herself a total mess she achieved a kind of unification. It may be the unification of failure, but that image is often easier to live with than the image of oneself as struggling and not succeeding. Most important, however, the thought she evoked was more ludicrous than tragic. "A total mess": the very phrase suggests a chaotic jumble, a roomful of disarray. It sounds exasperating but not fatal. In thus making light of her anguish, she created or attained what has been called "the god's-eye view"* of her predicament. She attained, that is, an objective, indifferent perspective on her suffering, wailing self.

At times of personal distress and, equally, at times of national tragedy and international horror (which, I guess, means pretty much at all times nowadays), this attainment is invaluable. It may not enable us to change reality, but it enables us to endure it. It may not allow us to discard our egos, but it allows us to transcend them. The full development of our sense of humor results in a frame of mind so free, so flexible, and so kaleidoscopic that it rigidifies nowhere, gets hooked on nothing. It results in a frame of mind so bold that it finds no creature and no institution sacred; a frame of mind so subtle that it discerns the irony that runs through all human affairs; a frame of mind so candid that it comprehends the hypocrisy of its candor; a frame of mind so indifferent that it has no more need of pride. It is this frame of mind that can, with some conviction, be called our ultimate hope, for the ability to evoke it represents an ability to take whatever comes with a shrug if not a smile.

Why then, to return to our original question, do we not fully cultivate it? What keeps this beautiful bud from flowering in all of us? The obstacles are implicit in the conditions we have discussed. If humor is release—release from our controls and inhibitions, from acceptance of the world at face value, and from identification with ourselves—the impediment to its unfolding is our fear of letting go. We are all

---

* I am indebted to D. H. Monro (*Argument of Laughter*, Melbourne University Press, 1951) for this felicitous phrase. It applies, as we will see, to our sense of humor's highest, most valuable, function. We will have occasion to refer to it more than once in the course of this study.

hung up somewhere along the line, if not in the earlier stages then in the more advanced ones and if not in those then certainly in our attachment to our selves. We all feel a need to bank on something or someone, to believe in something or someone, be it reason, morality, science, the church, democracy, family, friends, or our own attractiveness, intelligence, strength, or charm. These anchors provide our security; they keep us safely moored in the frightening swirl of being, but they thwart the full development of our capacity for humor. Our sense of humor is stunted, individually, by our personal security-blankets; it is stunted, collectively, by the fact that we crave security at all.

Some individuals, however, manage to develop this capacity to its uttermost extent. What enables them to do it? Ironically enough, two mutually contradictory conditions pave the way. On the one hand, utter nihilism allows certain people to scoff at everything, themselves included. Mark Twain, in his later years, fell into such a state of mind. The mood of his stories and sketches became increasingly bitter until, in the end, the creator of Huckleberry Finn could see man as nothing more than "a museum of diseases, a home of impurities," a creature who "begins as dirt and departs as stench." On the other hand, rare persons in every epoch have been able to relinquish their dependence on all tangible supports because they have made contact with an intangible souce of inspiration, a spring of vitality that seemingly depends on nothing but itself. In touch with such a source— call it God, the Oversoul, the Self—they disengage from all horrors, not in bitterness but in blitheness. James Thurber appears to have known this experience well. He was capable of perceiving his own worst tragedy in a humorous light. Suffering from encroaching blindness, for example, he wrote:

"It was in going over to Jersey that day, without my glasses, that I realized that the disadvantages of defective vision are at least partially compensated for by its peculiar advantages. Up to that time I had been in the habit of going to bed when my glasses were broken and lying there until they were fixed again. I had believed I could not go very far without them, not more than a block, anyway, on account of the danger of bumping into things, getting a headache, losing my way. None of those things happened, but a lot of others did. I saw the Cuban flag flying over a national bank, I saw a gay old lady with a gray parasol walk right through the side of a truck, I saw a cat roll across a street in a small striped barrel, I saw bridges rise lazily into the air, like balloons. . . . For the hawk-eyed person life has none of those soft edges which for me blur into fantasy; for such a person an electric welder is merely an electric welder, not a radiant fool setting off a sky-rocket by day. The kingdom of the partly blind is a little like Oz, a little like Wonderland, a little like Poictesme. Anything you can think of, and a lot you never would think of, can happen there."

The wounded-but-not-disheartened core of humor is an evanescent state of mind. Like a handful of sand, it slips through our fingers as we attempt to grasp it. Here and there, however, its spirit has been captured in images which we can contemplate. Another traditional Jewish story portrays it succinctly:

A wise old rabbi lay dying, so his disciples lined up next to his deathbed to catch his final words. They arranged themselves in order from the most brilliant pupil to the most obtuse. The brilliant one bent over the prostrate form and whispered, "Rabbi, rabbi. What are your final words?"

"My final words," murmured the ancient, "are . . . life is a river."

The disciple passed it on to the fellow next to him and the phrase traveled like wildfire down the line. "The rabbi says life is a river." . . . "The rabbi says life is a river." . . . "The rabbi says life is a river."

When it reached the oaf at the end, however, he scratched his head in perplexity. "What does the rabbi mean, life is a river?" he asked.

That question, of course, traveled back up the line. "What does the rabbi mean, life is a river?" "What does the rabbi mean, life is a river?"

When the star pupil heard it, he leaned over again. "Rabbi," he implored, for the old man was breathing his last, "What do you mean, life is a river?"

And the wise one, shrugging, croaked, "So it's not a river!"

Let us try to absorb his message, for, in that final moment, that rabbi displayed the very soul of humor.

Freedom
from
Conformity

The fundamental social bond from which humor frees us is the bond of conformity—the compulsion to act, think, and feel in ways which are sanctioned by our group. Comic figures throughout history defy this bond. They engage in behavior which is deemed inappropriate, improper, or positively scandalous by their society. So doing, they delight their countrymen no end.

Trickster,* an American Indian folk-hero, amused his audience by acts which were unheard of in their culture. An ostensible man of peace, he conducted war; a professed friend of animals, he secretly devoured them; a lusty male, he sometimes transformed himself into a female. His adventures

---

* His exploits are described in detail by Paul Radin in *The Trickster*, Routledge and Kegan Paul, 1956.

were notably risqué; in one of the more imaginative, he directed his penis to sneak into the chief's daughter as she was bathing in a stream, while the rest of him remained hidden and prepared to enjoy the encounter in safety.

He may seem bizarre to us, but this character struck the early Indians as hilarious. Impulsive, irrational, and immoral, he broke all their tribal taboos and disregarded all their principles of decent living. He was capable of almost anything—and that, in its primitive essense, is the genuine spirit of humor.

The Marx Brothers' movies, to come closer to our own experience, purvey the same sort of basic, unsophisticated comedy. They relate to our culture much as Trickster did to his, for in scene after scene they manage to despoil the traditions we conventionally accept. Whether through disruption of the pious atmosphere attending a performance of the opera or the insane ingenuity of squeezing lemonade with their bare feet, they make a shambles of what we consider respectable behavior.

Picture Trickster's penis swimming slyly to its goal or, if you take your imagery less raw, picture Groucho striding through polite society shocking everyone in reach, and you have an action-portrait of the ludicrous at work.

Peruse the delightful cartoon on the next page.

The enterprising orderly delights us by behaving in a socially outrageous manner. What he does is amusing because it is so nonconforming, true to impulse, and distinct from the conventional role of the hospital employee.

All human beings, from primitive to present times, have guffawed at the spectacle of nonconformity. Why? Simply because we have all been enjoined to conform. Every social

group, from the smallest family or friendship circle to the largest national or international organization, exerts an influence on its members to comply with its particular standards. The fact is well known; to dwell on it may seem gratuitous; yet we generally see it operating only on other people. While accepting the fact in principle, most of us cherish the conceit that our own behavior is determined by personal choice. In all innocence, we feed on the illusion that the ways we live are the results of thoughtful decisions or natural inclinations. Blind as we may keep ourselves, however, the truth is that from infancy to the grave we are pushed, pulled, seduced, and coerced by group pressures which obliterate our inclinations and nullify our uniqueness, so that on the whole the vast majority of us live standardized, preprocessed lives. Our manner of dress, our manner of speech, our eating and sleeping habits, the ways and places and times in which we work, play, love, and hate: every aspect of our existence, from the most trivial to the most profound, is molded by group expectations. It should come as no surprise, then, that the sight of a comic ignoring conventions excites us. We exult in his brash impertinence because it provides us, vicariously, a moment of freedom from the prisons of our own adjustments.

Were we to dare it ourselves, we could experience that much more of the thrill, but we are either intimidated or so thoroughly brainwashed that, as adults, we hardly remember how to be spontaneous. Let any one of us defy convention to the point of wading in a public fountain on a hot summer day or wearing jeans to a wedding or a funeral and the onlookers will, in all likelihood, regard him as a "kook." Only if it is clearly defined as a joke can we allow ourselves the luxury of enjoying it, and even then most of us content ourselves with remaining spectators. To perform an unconventional act on impulse—to do it just for the hell of it—seems too bold or too imaginative to try.

Those who have tried it, however, know the invigorating joy it brings. In classes I have taught on humor, there has often been a joker who would recall, with glee, a number of scandalous exploits in which he had participated. Serving laxatives to unsuspecting guests, appearing nude in a public place, falling asleep and snoring at a lecture, or simply walking out on a job, with no explanation, to spend a few days at the beach: such renegade acts have given great pleasure to those who have dared them.

The vast majority of us, nevertheless, consider our impulses too irresponsible, too childish to indulge in. So we hew the line. We get up in the morning, brush our teeth, drink our coffee, drive to our place of employment, and proceed—just like a hundred million others—through the paces that our social milieu has prescribed. We fail to recognize the extent to which our uniqueness has been stifled, but we sense it dumbly, dimly, in the deadening monotony of our days. The predictable routine brings sterility, lassitude, a restless mood of unfulfillment. We feel only half alive.

In this stifling atmosphere, comedy supplies a breath of fresh air by revealing possibilities we normally censor from our repertoires. By aping its example, by behaving now and then like a buffoon, a joker, or a clown, we could inject ourselves with the excitement the comic bestows. But we rarely dare to do it. The question is why. Is it only fear and habit that hold us back, or are there more intrinsic reasons for remaining square?

Unfortunately—since it complicates our topic, not to say our lives, no end—we must admit the latter. Contrary to the claims of radical dreamers, we experience not just a diminution of ourselves in our conventional routines but, paradoxically, an enhancement too. In relinquishing the random play of impulse, we acquire skills and knowledge, and all the cynicism in the world cannot deny the satisfaction to be gleaned from such accomplishment. All pleas for spontaneity notwithstanding, it is futile to disclaim the pleasure of learning to play the piano, mastering the potter's wheel, or comprehending the strategies of chess—yet the achievement of these ends inevitably demands the surrender of our whims to a regime of concentrated effort.

Even more important, making spontaneity a conscious goal is an intrinsically dubious venture. How can we decide to "let go" when the essence of the act is that it is not decided upon? Like laughter, it occurs; it is not done. If we try to do it, if we try to be spontaneous, we strike ourselves out before we have stepped up to the plate.

An illustration of this dilemma is provided by all bohemian and hippie groups. Beginning as a reaction to stifling social conditions, as a quest for renewed vitality through non-conformity, they degenerate into cults as soon as their aims are formulated. Still subject, as we all are, to the needs they sought to escape, they band together into subcultures as conformist as the parent culture from which they rebelled. Their distinctive jargon, clothing, hairstyles, occupations, and activities are adhered to ritualistically; their values and antipathies are shared by one and all. Originating in the matrix of the spirit of liberation, they end by becoming its butt.

Observations such as these are generally made with the intention of discrediting dissident movements, but this intention in itself is pitifully narrow-minded. It fails—as the hippies themselves fail—to grasp the essential point of the whole dilemma. We must dissent, and we cannot dissent. We must break free of tribal taboos, yet all we can do is exchange one set of taboos for another set. We simply do not know how to define ourselves except in relation to other members of our species. If we reject, therefore, the standards of one group, we will soon accept the standards of another.

The moment of change is a moment of heightened self-awareness, but that moment is, and will always be, fleeting.

The spirit of humor is synonymous with that moment. It is iconoclastic. It is rebellious, but in an individual—not a group—sense. Its joy is the joy of release, and release is exciting only as reaction to the constricting conditions out of which it is born. Those who attempt to exist in a state of sustained disinhibition soon find their paradise fading. They are then compelled to employ artificial means, to engage in more and more desperate measures to repeat the excitement they originally achieved so naturally.

The dynamics of humor illuminate this problem, for laughter obeys the same laws as other forms of emotional release. Pick up any large collection of jokes or cartoons and I defy you to continue to laugh when you are halfway through. The same is true of an uninterrupted comic recital. We may roar with genuine delight for a while but, if the quips continue without letup, we will soon be reduced to grinning in frozen mirth: unable to laugh, lucky to chuckle, and rather weary at the end. The point is that our conventional view of life must be repeatedly reestablished so that we can enjoy release from it again and again.

To begin to cultivate our own sense of humor, *we need to become elastic with regard to society's demands*. Neither to stay prisoner to them nor to discard them: that is the goal. Wedded to conformity, we sink into banality; divorced, we end up in the grip of an alternate system. If we acquire, however, the frame of mind in which humor flourishes—the individual, iconoclastic outlook—we will have set ourselves on a springboard to freedom. If we allow ourselves to challenge all the shibboleths by which we live, to question all the

verities of our society, to abrogate, when we feel the urge, all
the standard practices of all the groups to which we belong,
we will rediscover the exuberance we knew as children, rekindle the spark of Trickster and Groucho in our lives.

But let us not delude ourselves so early in the game. This
prescription, like all good advice, is easy to give and hard to
take. If we think we can readily adopt it or, more likely, if
we secretly believe we already practice it, that only goes to
show how much we have to learn. The true nonconformist is
a rare and wondrous bird. Were his species as numerous as
our claims might indicate, we would have no political parties,
no religions, no armies, and no schools of thought on any
subject whatsoever. Individual nonconformity is as slippery
as a piece of ice in our sweaty little hands. Luckily, however,
there is no need to imprison it. What we must, and can, do to
cultivate our sense of humor is reach out for it again and
again. Reach out and let it enter. Let the spirit of our purely
individual, asocial, natural impulses wash over us and re-
awaken us from our sweet, cozy dreams of security.

Freedom
from
Inferiority

One of the most miserable conditions that can afflict a human being is the feeling of being inferior or inadequate. When we perceive ourselves as less intelligent, less attractive, less successful, than those about us or, on a subtler level, when we find ourselves falling short of our own personal standards, we are all depressed and agitated. Anyone who suffers from a severe inferiority complex is a woeful, pitiful creature, and the average man, in his moments of self-belittlement, is equally distressed.

Our sense of humor, however, strengthens our ability to cope with this condition. It accomplishes the task in two ways: by degrading those who augment our inferiority and by deriding the entire enterprise of "getting ahead." Let us examine each in turn.

The Lone Ranger and his sidekick, Tonto, ride to the top of a hill overlooking the plains. Peering round, the masked man exclaims, "There are hostile Indians approaching from the south!"
"Then we will ride to the north, kemo saby," replies his loyal friend.
"But there are also hostile Indians approaching from the north."
"Then we will ride to the west, kemo saby."
"I'm afraid we can't, for there are hostile Indians approaching from the west, too."
"Then we will ride to the east, kemo saby."
"But, but there are also hostile Indians approaching from the east!"
"Well, so long—white man!"

Our enjoyment of this interchange stems from its portrayal of the underdog becoming top dog, the minority coming into a position of strength. The racial undertones of "so long—white man" are hardly muted, but even though we may be white we still identify with Tonto, for in one way or another we all experience ourselves as underdogs to someone in power.

Retaliatory wit such as this is prevalent in every culture, every country. Its targets are those persons or groups who exercise power: the government, the police, the rich, the famous, the influential, the learned. In Hungary, for example, the populace trades anecdotes about their policemen which, with little or no modification, any nation might apply to theirs. Thus, as they say in Budapest:

Here the policemen always travel in pairs. For efficiency—because, if they're lucky, one can read and one can write.

Or again:

The teacher is questioning a group of primary school pupils about their aim in life. "And what do you want to be when you grow up,

Johnny?" she asks.
  "I want to be a doctor."
  "That's nice. How old are you now?"
  "Ten years old."
  "And what do you want to be when you grow up, Paul?"
  "I want to be an engineer."
  "Good. And how old are you?"
  "Eleven years old."
  "And Michael, what do you want to be when you grow up?"
  "I want to be a policeman."
  "Oh, that's fine. And how old are you now?"
  "I dunno."

In similar fashion, every downtrodden group in the world uses wit as a weapon to strike back at its oppressors. Children mock their parents, students satirize their teachers, employees lampoon their employers. We all derive a salient satisfaction from the exercise of ridiculing our superiors because it allows us to throw off the feeling of inferiority their power instils in us. In showing them up as stupid, selfish, mean or conceited, or in creating a fantasy wherein the victors become the victims, we provide ourselves a moment of respite from our subordinated condition.

We all love to do it. We love it even more, however, if the underdog does not just upset his oppressor any way at all but employs the oppressor's own momentum as leverage with which to do him in.

A little Jew in Hitler's Germany brushes by a Nazi officer, knocking him off balance. "Schwein!" roars the Nazi, clicking his heels imperiously. To which the Jew, undaunted, makes a low bow and replies, "Cohen. Pleased to meet you."

The oppressor here is hoisted by his own petard; his own

expletive is used against him and, on account of that, the joke deals out an extra measure of satisfaction. Similarly, we might laugh at the gumption of a Jew who took occasion to kick Hermann Goering in the pants, but the act would be even more delightful if the Field Marshal had bent over first, exposing himself to the attack.

Retaliatory wit is improved to the extent that it follows naturally from its target's position, to the extent that he lays himself open for it. Take this beautifully concise scene as a further illustration:

> *Two men are conversing at a cocktail party. "See those two gorgeous women over there?" the first man boasts. "Well, one is my wife and the other is my mistress." To which his companion replies, "You took the words right out of my mouth."*

We appreciate the fact that the bigshot gets his come-uppance, but we enjoy it the more because in his very boast he has set himself up for the shaft.

Here is yet another variation on the theme:

> *The doctor's wife is unable to sleep because the toilet is dripping. So she has her husband call the plumber in the middle of the night. After listening to the problem on the phone, the plumber grumpily declares, "But it's 2 A.M.!"*
>
> *"So what?" replies the doctor. "If your child was sick, wouldn't you call me?"*
>
> *"Yes," mumbles the plumber. "You're right. So I'll tell you what to do. Throw a couple of aspirins into the bowl and, if it doesn't get better by morning, call me again."*

The superior individual has not just been toppled from his perch; he has been done in with his own weapons.

Psychologically, such stories satisfy our wish for revenge and assuage our potential guilt in one swoop. We need not feel we have committed an act of unwarranted malice in outwitting either the boaster or the doctor, for we have simply utilized their own machinations as wires to trip them up. By twisting the oppressor's characteristics against him, the underdog achieves a moment of unadulterated glory. While revenge may be sweet, justified revenge is whipped cream with the cherry on top.

All the foregoing jokes make their assaults directly, setting up their particular target and subjecting him to ridicule. Of greater interest, however, is the technique of indirect humorous attack. Here the wit constructs a scene in which he behaves toward himself as his oppressor does, but even more so. By parodying the oppressor's attitudes, he insinuates their absurdity. Negro comics, for example, tell the following story:

A little Negro girl smears her face with white cold cream. Running to her mother in the kitchen, she exclaims, "Mommy, Mommy, look at me!"

The mother replies with an angry "Get that gunk off your face!"

The child scurries to her father, but the same interchange occurs. Downcast and pouting, she returns to the bathroom, muttering, "I haven't been white for more than five minutes and already I hate two niggers."

In similar vein, workers raise a laugh by mimicking the boss berating them, students the teacher lecturing them, army privates the sergeant bellowing at them. So doing, they all achieve a sense of release from their subordinate roles. Let us consider why, for in the exploration of this maneuver we will come upon a crucial discovery.

Several factors are at work. In the first place, adopting the expressions of our superiors gives us the illusion of stepping across the line, of actually becoming "big shot" for a while. No matter that our reason knows it is not so; role-playing, like daydreaming, helps us feel better than reality permits. At the same time, the stories through which we parody our over-lords expose the stupidity on which their domination rests. The childish reactions that give rise to racial prejudice, for instance, are revealed in the anecdote related above, and when we mimic our bosses, teachers, and sergeants, we use intonations or gestures that convey their imbecility in treat-ing us the way they do. Most important, however, is the fact that *the very act of making fun of our inferior position raises us above it.* This is true not only of subordinated social status but of all inferiorities of any kind. The laughter with which we mock our weaknesses asserts that while we suffer them we also transcend them, look down on them from a height, make light of them, and thus live on enjoyably despite them.

An old Jew is dying. His family crowds round the deathbed. In a parched, feeble voice, the old man inquires, "Is Sara here?"
"Yes, darling," his wife sobs.
"Is Morris here?"
"Yes, Dad," his son replies.
"Is Judith here?"
"Yes, Daddy," his daughter whispers.
"Oy vey!" he groans. "So who's taking care of the store?"

An all-Jewish jury is trying a case. They deliberate their verdict and return to the courtroom. "Mr. Foreman," the judge demands, "has the jury reached a verdict?"
"Well, your Honor," the foreman replies, "we have discussed the matter from all angles. Mr. Levy felt it was a shame the crime was committed and Mrs. Goldberg thought the defendant was such a nice boy. Then Mr. Finkelstein reminded us . . ."

"Yes yes," the judge interrupts. "But what is your verdict?"
"Our verdict," the foreman declares, "is we shouldn't mix in."

Are these jokes self-disparaging? Is the Jew who makes fun of his idiosyncracies a masochist? Is he motivated, as some so-called experts have claimed, by a need to feel humiliated? Nonsense! Jewish laughter at jests such as these is evidence not of masochism but of expanded perspective, of what D. H. Monro has called "the god's-eye view."* It is evidence of the mental act of rising above one's deficiencies by frankly admitting and enjoying them.

In those remarkable instances—be they traditional jokes, current quips, or personal observations—in which people see themselves naked and smile, in which they expose their own oddity and laugh at it, we unearth the root system of humor's therapeutic power. When all else fails, man has the capacity to picture his plight as part of the absurdity, the gross injustice of human affairs and in so doing to become a free, detached observer of his fate.

Heywood Broun, according to legend,** invested forty years' accumulated savings in the stock market and lost it all in the crash of 1929. His reaction, when he heard the news, was "Easy come; easy go."

The victim who, like Broun, laughs at his own tragedy, is a victor conquering his tragedy. This holds true for every person who feels defeated or inferior in any way. There need be no exquisite pain involved, no guilt-absolving suffering or other neurotic mechanisms. The experience need only be one

---

* See the earlier note on page 30.
** It is related by his friend, Corey Ford, in *The Time of Laughter,* Little, Brown, and Co., 1967.

of sudden mental expansion, of standing outside oneself and marveling at one's wounds, to result in a moment of mirth that affirms, inarticulately, the natural joy of being.

❦ Therein lies the genius of our human equipment. We can free ourselves from feelings of inadequacy by the simple expedient of laughing off our lacks. We can rise above our failures by the exercise of our sense of humor. Why, then, do we do it so infrequently? If the solution to our distress is practically within our grasp, why don't we pick it up?

The question is moot, but the answer seems to revolve around our common tendency to identify with our tangible, demonstrable qualities. If the items that matter most in our estimation of ourselves are the amount of money we possess, the accomplishments we can list, the attractiveness of our physiques, the prestige we enjoy among our contemporaries, we will be hard put to make light of our faults and failings. If, on the other hand, we value our essential, intangible being above all our lesser attributes, we can more easily accept defeat without discouragement.

Exercising our sense of humor in this respect, then, involves a shift of values from the materialistic to the non-materialistic plane. The extent to which we are willing to relinquish our greedy needs determines the extent to which we can overcome our inferiority feelings through humor.

We have focused so far on our experience in being subjugated by others, our need for retaliation and reviving self-esteem, and the ways in which humor can help us in these circumstances. Subjugation, however, is not by any means the sole condition through which inferiority feelings arise. Subtler, but more damaging in the long run, is our comparison of our characteristics and accomplishments with our own ideals.

The man who frequently falls short of his own expectations cannot help but be distressed. Entire lives, in fact, are soured by this simple disparity: his ego does not match his ego-ideal, so all a man's virtues go unrecognized. No matter that he has a pleasant disposition, a reliable, trustworthy character, a keen mind, a good heart—if he cannot live up to the standards he sets for himself, he sulks, becomes irritable, and gnashes his teeth in frustration.

The pattern is all too common, and it leads at times not just to unpleasant but even to tragic results. In our frustration with ourselves, we are prone to attack those we love, to destroy friendships and marriages, to hate life instead of appreciating it. The cause appears to be rooted in the fact that we live in a highly competitive society, a milieu where we are pressed from every side to get ahead. Most of us internalize this directive early and come to expect substantial achievements from ourselves. Then, if we fail to produce them, we either conclude that we are inferior or, in our desperation, blame everyone and everything around us for holding us back.

We have only to examine the situation for a moment, though, to ask whether all the struggle and rush is worth the effort. Is accomplishment really conducive to personal happiness? It hardly seems to be, since the indices of mal-contentment—neurosis, suicide, divorce—are as prevalent among successful persons as among the unsuccessful. In this light it would not be difficult to argue a case for relinquishing ambition, for reverting to a casual, happy-go-lucky frame of mind. Strive for nothing beyond our most basic necessities, we could tell ourselves, and we will avoid frustration and disappointment.

But there is a joker in the deck. The undeniable fact of the matter is that material and prestige rewards await the victors in society's competitive pursuits, and we dearly love those rewards. Besides that, there is a keen pleasure to be had from improvement and accomplishment themselves—the pleasure of achieving mastery, of experiencing oneself as competent—and once we have known that pleasure we will not willingly forgo it.

Our predicament, in short, is intrinsically ironic, for our ambitions lead us into both gratification and misery: The same set of motives, in other words, sets us up simultaneously for fulfillment and failure. Many humorists have commented on this impossible state of affairs. Swift, Cervantes, Molière, Twain: the greatest wits of all nations have observed both the folly of striving and the folly of failing to strive.

In *As You Like It*, act 2, Shakespeare juxtaposes two pretty songs on this theme. First, all the forest inhabitants sing,

> *Who doth ambition shun*
> *And loves to live i' th' sun,*
> *Seeking the food he eats,*
> *And pleased with what he gets,*
> *Come hither, come hither, come hither.*
> *Here shall he see no enemy*
> *But winter and rough weather.*

A moment later, Jaques, the sardonic malcontent, adds,

> *If it do come to pass*
> *That any man turn ass,*
> *Leaving his wealth and ease*

A stubborn will to please,
Ducdame, ducdame, ducdame.
Here shall he see gross fools as he,
An if he will come to me.

The wisdom, then, of shunning the "rat race" of civilization and retiring to a simpler way of life is both extolled and
mocked. We know it, too, from our own experience: the
pleasure and the boredom of the simple life, the ease and the
ennui of relinquishing all ambitions.

James Thurber, in our own time, toyed with this dilemma
more than once, depicting in lucid imagery the ironic crux of
the matter. In his fable "The Shrike and the Chipmunks,"
for example, a male chipmunk who fiddles his time away
making artistic designs with nuts and sleeping all day and
never doing his duties is berated by his wife. "You can't be
healthy if you lie in bed all day and never get any exercise,"
she tells him. So he gets up and goes for a walk with her in
the sunlight and they are killed by a shrike. Thurber codas
the tale with this moral: "Early to rise and early to bed
makes a male healthy and wealthy and dead."

The fable clearly suggests that our accepted codes of work-
aday behavior are asinine. Through Thurber's whimsy, we are
brought to question the value we place on persevering labor.
Light as the touch may be, it mocks the social code that
causes the dreamers and putterers among us to doubt themselves, to rate themselves inferior because they cannot apply
their energies to what the rest of us consider essential tasks.

In the final analysis, the humorous view almost always
pronounces judgment against ambition—be it materialistic,

intellectual, or spiritual. Thus, a fine story* tells of a college graduate who, having attained all possible academic honors, remained dissatisfied because he still did not know the meaning of life:

He determined to seek out the wisest philosophers in the world and ask them. This he did, but none could impart the answer. After years of travel and inquiry, however, he met a Hindu mystic in Tibet who said, "I too do not know the meaning of life—but I know who knows!" The young man was aflame with excitement and, when he learned that the one who knew lived atop a mountain in perpetual contemplation, he could not wait to search him out. Accordingly, he made the treacherous ascent, dangerous beyond imagination, and finally, exhausted and bleeding, arrived at the knower's cave.

The ancient, emaciated seer turned to him in silence. On the young man's pallid brow he could read the burning question. Nodding, he moved his lips. "Life," the hollow voice intoned, "is a river."

"A river?" The seeker was beside himself. "A river!! That's sophomoric philosophizing! I heard that one back at college! How can you say that life is a river?"

"You mean," the ancient rejoined in shattering dismay, "you mean—it isn't?"

Humor reveals the fatuity of inferiority feelings based on lack of achievement by calling into question the very pursuit of achievement itself. Whether our goal is knowledge, wealth, power, or fame, the comic spirit undercuts its worth. "What's the point?" it jeers. "No final answers are attainable, no accomplishments enduring, no positions unassailable. So admit it: wouldn't we be far better off in a cozy bed, engaging in pleasant pastimes and dozing, intermittently, to wake to more of the same?"

---

* It is a variation on the Jewish story we discussed earlier (pp. 32-33) and shows, among other things, the very different effects achieved by a switch of punch lines capping the same basic theme.

Our sense of humor frees us from inferiority by degrading both our superiors and the quest for superiority itself. To facilitate it, we must become more willing to accept its essential outlook. We must recognize and remember that the rich, the powerful, the learned, the successful, are riddled with as many flaws as we, and we must admit that the struggle for riches, power, knowledge, or prestige is at best a dubious venture.

The extent to which we can sustain this outlook is the extent to which we can cultivate this branch of our sense of humor. Each time we become amused at the spectacle of competitive behavior, each time we acknowledge the absurdity of feeling less or more worthwhile than anyone else, we bleach our inferiority complexes and bolster our acceptance of ourselves.

The game of indulging in this kind of humor can be highly rewarding. It can pay off with freedom from all feelings of inadequacy, which is surely no meager stake. Valuable as it can be, however, the exercise can be learned too well. For the individual who goes beyond coping with his inferiority feelings and eradicates them completely turns out, in the end, to be an ass. Inferiority, after all, is akin to humility. A man may be foolish to conceive of himself as more imperfect than his neighbor or to berate himself for not having attained perfection, but he is equally foolish if he thinks he has attained it.

The psychiatrist is addressing his patient. "You don't have an inferiority complex," he says. "Your problem is—you are inferior."

Like almost every anecdote, this story can be appreciated on more than one level. We may enjoy the unexpected candor of the doctor; we may revel in the glory of seeing some poor shnook put down. If, however, in our amusement we recognize ourselves in that poor shnook, we sip the story to its dregs. We see, for the moment at least, that inferiority is not just a problem to be gotten rid of; it is a fact of life, an ineradicable aspect of our existence, an awareness to contend with forever.

Our sense of humor encourages us to accept our imperfections, not to deny them: to accept them because they are ours, like our children are ours, because they are part of us, part of our life, because they help define our uniqueness and link us to all humanity. When we love ourselves in our awkwardness, our ugliness, we have nothing more to envy. We are freed from inferiority by the expedient of embracing our inferiority.

Why, then, don't we do it? Why don't we incorporate this liberating outlook? We may claim that what we most desire is contentment with ourselves, but the facts deny it. The manner in which we live our lives suggests that other, darker desires are stronger, for the majority of us spend little time treading this pathway to self-acceptance.

We speculated earlier that the problem revolves around our common inclination to identify with our tangible characteristics rather than our essential, intangible self. It appears to revolve, too, around our legitimate need to assert our powers, to validate our existence, to manifest ourselves as competent, worthwhile creatures in the world. This need can never be denied. For the sake of our mental health, it must never be denied. And yet, on the face of it, what our sense of humor requires is acceptance of our incompetence, our worthlessness, our powerlessness, as the precondition to attaining a state of being no worldly force can destroy.

In the early days of the cinema, Charlie Chaplin created a comic character who brilliantly embodied all the qualities we are laboring to define. The epitome of the "little guy"—weak, nervous, poor, and alone—he always managed to rise above adversity, to give his superiors their licks, and, without denying or disguising his own frailties, to sustain a jaunty air of self-assurance. Within and despite his impoverished condition, the Chaplin character had *joie de vivre*. He never fell prey to egotistical conceit, but nothing could destroy his innate dignity. To nurture that part of our own sense of humor that is concerned with overcoming inferiority feelings, we could not do better than to take Charlie Chaplin as a guiding image.

Freedom from Morality

Humor breaks us free from our moral inhibitions in at least two ways. It allows us to indulge both our sexual promiscuity and our callous disregard for other people's feelings. Since sex and viciousness comprise the two major streams of impulse we normally try to control, it should come as no surprise to find that they fuel our gustiest laughter. To fertilize our sense of humor, however, we must become more receptive to these streams of impulse in general. Recognizing them as normal, vital parts of our human equipment, seeing them as necessary to our well-being, provides the groundwork on which our enjoyment can be erected.

Ribald humor draws its sustenance from two main sources: sexual behavior and elimination of body wastes. Both, as we know, are activities conducted in private in our society and both form the subject matter for innumerable titillating jests.

The connection is obvious. Enjoined by our moral code to keep our sexual practices discreet and to make no public mention of our eleminative needs, we cherish the opportunity to display them both in fun. Bawdy sketches and remarks allow us to share our stifled interest in the physiological facts of life. They free us from the armor of our modesty and bid us loll about in naked ease.

The earliest obscenity in our culture occurs at the nursery-school level. Here, to our amusement or chagrin, we can find three- and four-year-olds whispering "doo-doo" or "wee-wee" and giggling delightedly. These children have absorbed the notion that toilet activities are not to be discussed in public and their testing the taboo affords them great enjoyment.

A few years later, we may hear elementary-school pupils reciting verses like the following:

> *As I sat under the apple tree,*
> *A birdie sent his love to me,*
> *And as I wiped it from my eye,*
> *I said—thank goodness cows can't fly!*

The naughty reference, we can see, has been developed into a full-fledged joke.

Through adolescence, scatological or toilet humor flourishes, finding expression in coarse, earthy slang, insulting gestures, boorish stories, conundrums, and tongue-twisters. Frequently, now, the intention of the jest is also hostile: to degrade or make a fool of whoever the butt may be.*

---

* Try repeating this pattern ten times, fast:
    One smart feller, he felt smart;
    Two smart fellers, they felt smart;
    Three smart fellers, they felt smart . . .
See what I mean?

In adulthood, the emphasis on anal functions diminishes, but it never completely disappears. Toilet humor of one sort or another is indulged in at all ages. Its wittiness, however, is generally feeble, for while it is true that with discussion of our toilet functions being discouraged in polite society, we gain a moment of relief by making reference to them in public, the intensity of the relief is minimal since, as adults, we harbor little guilt or anxiety in this area.

Not all jokes with an anal reference, however, are concerned with elimination proper. Many times the reference is incidental, while the thrust of the story points to a competitive aspect of human relations. Take the one about the sailor and his two captains:

This particular sailor was a good man on a ship, but he had one infuriating quality: he never lost a bet. So finally, after years of losing money to him, his captain decided to get rid of him. Another ship needed a mate, so he arranged for a transfer, warning the new captain, however, of the man's uncanny luck.

"Be careful," he said. "Don't ever make a bet with that guy, 'cause you'll be sure to lose."

"Thanks for the tip," replied the other captain. "I'll remember."

Well, the first night out the new captain started complaining about his hemorrhoids. "They're so painful," he moaned, "I can hardly sit down."

And sure enough, up spoke the sailor. "I know a cure for hemorrhoids and I'll bet you fifty dollars it works."

"Oh yah?" said the captain, suspiciously. "What is it?"

"When you go to bed tonight, just insert a ripe banana in your rectum, and you'll see—by tomorrow morning you'll be cured."

Now the captain had not attained to his position by accident. He was a shrewd man, and he thought: Here's a perfect bet. If I lose, as I have been warned, my piles will be cured, and that's worth fifty dollars any time. On the other hand, if his advice is no good and I win, I'll have beaten this supposedly unbeatable smart aleck. So either way I've got to come out on top.

Accordingly, he accepted the bet and agreed to try the sailor's remedy.

Next morning, of course, he awoke in worse pain than ever, and immediately hobbled over to the mate to tell him so. Shrugging, the man handed over his fifty.

Naturally, when they got back to port, the first thing the captain did was rush over to the other captain to tell him the news. But when he heard it, the poor man suffered a conniption fit. "No," he whimpered. "No, no, no. I can't stand it! I can't!! Do you know what that guy said to me as he was transferring from my ship to yours? He said, 'Captain, I'll bet you a thousand dollars'—and of course I took him up on it— 'that my new captain is so dumb that before we return to port I'll talk him into shoving a banana up his ass!' "

Dealing as it does in double trickery, this story makes its impact on a basis beyond the piquant. Its intention is clearly retaliatory. By developing a scene in which a little guy outwits his superiors and humiliates them to boot, it would amuse us even without its ribaldry. Most important, however, it illustrates the increase in humorous potential a joke acquires as it delves into interpersonal relationships. While the ludicrous may be evoked in solitary acts, it is amplified by setting those acts into a context of human interaction, for human interaction is the locus of our most acute anxieties, most rife hypocrisies, and most ridiculous illusions.

Physical exposure brings us closer to this level of meaningful relationships, though in itself it does not quite achieve it. Mere reference to private body parts makes children titter, and many adolescents, uncomfortably conscious of their budding bodies, find nudity jokes highly gratifying too, but the concerns and conflicts of most adults have advanced beyond the stage at which they can feel fulfilled by a look at a naked epidermis.

I don't want to sell it short, for it does break us free from a restriction we normally observe and, prior to the attain ment of senility or sainthood as the case may be, it activates a lurking libidinal impulse we all share; but in the long run the focus on physique alone, like the focus on elimination alone, is too banal to provide much richness of humorous pleasure. When the focus is widened enough to include a satirical comment on human relationships, however, we can all enjoy it fully. Consider this cartoon:

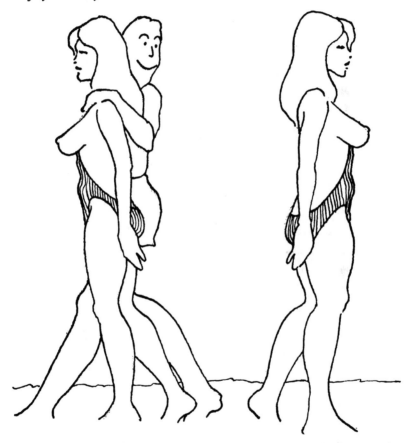

Beginning as an exercise in voyeurism, it culminates in an incisive observation on human behavior. It leaves us enlightened as well as aroused, for it provides a glimpse into the irony of everyday life.

Cartoons like this approach the finest in risqué fare. They raise the level of ribaldry to the status of instant philosophy. It is only when we come to stories dealing directly with sexual relations, however, that the essence of the ribald is distilled. Sexual jokes may range from stupid to brilliant and from delicate to coarse, but weaving them together is a common denominator of basic psychological significance. Let us try to discern it.

A young monk who lived in Siberia,
Found life growing drearia and drearia,
So he did to a nun
What he shouldn't have done—
And now she's a Mother Superia.

A princess wandering in the fields comes upon an ugly, croaking frog. When it sees her, it speaks up in a resonant voice, saying, "Don't be afraid of me. I am really a handsome prince, but a wicked witch has put me under this curse. You can save me, though. If you will only take me to bed with you for one night, I will be transformed into my natural self."

The princess has many misgivings, but she determines to do it anyway. So she takes the frog to bed with her and, in the morning, opens her eyes to see the handsome prince. Unfortunately, he is still a frog, and ugly as ever.

"What is the meaning of this?" she exclaims. "I thought you told me . . ."

"Princess," interjects the frog, shrugging. "Princess—you've been screwed."

An adolescent boy is suffering the discomfort of a continual erection. Not knowing what to do about it, he decides to consult a doctor. As luck would have it, the doctor is out, but the nurse asks him what his problem is. When he tells her, she takes pity on him and says, "Lie down on this couch. I'll treat your ailment for you." And she does so, and the boy is very happy.

On leaving, he asks her the fee. "Five dollars," she replies. So he pays her and leaves.

A week later he is back with the same complaint. This time, however, the doctor is in. When he hears the problem, he says, "Lie down here and we'll put an ice pack on it." They proceed to do so and, in a little while, the boy is ready to go home.

"How much is the fee?" he asks.

"Two dollars," replies the doctor.

"Thank you," he says, paying up. "But there's one thing I want to tell you before I leave."

"Yes, of course. What is it?"

The patient fixes him with an acrid glance. "Cheap is cheap," he says, slamming the door behind him.

What do all these lewd tales have in common? What outlook do they all convey? Beyond their subsidiary innuendos (for instance the limerick's slur at Catholicism), they suggest, it should be clear, a distinct and disturbing view of sex. Gently or crudely, they all propose the view that the sexual drive is no more refined, no more meaningful, than an itch. In this outlook, they join forces with every ribald anecdote the world has ever known. Copulation, according to the dirty joke, is neither beautiful nor tender, but simply carnal and mechanical. The aim of heterosexual relations, obscenity implies, is to obtain satisfaction as cheaply as possible, to get away with it any way we can. In stories of this caliber, the so-called act of love is robbed of all affection. It is presented as a furtive drive, and a mockery is made of those romantic pretensions with which we normally endow it.

Why then do we smile in satisfaction, laugh in glee? What pleasure do we get from savoring this attitude? These questions bring us to the heart of the matter. And the truth is (who will deny it?) that we smile and laugh because we are found out, because we are touched at our core, because the implicit message of the dirty joke rings true and enables us, for a delicious, fleeting moment, to stop pretending, stop striving and hoping and dreaming, and to fall back honestly into our flesh and bones. All ribaldry delivers us from the modesty that checks the joy of our sensuous being, but stories dwelling on sexual relations grab us in the quick. By portraying copulation as a casual, self-indulgent, biological affair, they free us from the most trying demand we place on ourselves: the demand for closeness, for intimacy, for relatedness—the demand, in short, for love.

Much as we crave the sincere devotion of romantic sexual involvement, we also seek to avoid it. We find life barren without it, yet we find it difficult to endure. We pine for our own true love but, having secured it, we begin to hanker for promiscuous adventures. This is the irony on which bawdy humor thrives. The tug-of-war between our hunger for intimacy and our appetite for fornicating is intrinsic to our nature, even though the balance may shift, as the years roll by, from the pulsating lust for a lay to the gentle reaching out for love.

Ribald laughter is a blend of humor and pornography. Its appeal is based on both these elements; its message, while coherent, is twofold. As humor it advises us to take our morals, our modesty, and especially our need for love with a grain of salt. Let us not, it exhorts, beguile ourselves with romantic illusions—or if we do, let us retain the capacity to shuck them off in the end. As pornography it suggests that we ordinary, clean-living citizens could rejuvenate ourselves by rediscovering the sweet pungent wildness of the flesh.

Clutch, squeeze, and celebrate the pleasures of the moment, it prescribes—for the moment, the present moment, is all we know for sure. Sex for the fun of it, sex for the hell of it: these are the attitudes we must be willing to subscribe to—or at least to indulge in from time to time—if we wish to allow the ribald stream of humor to enrich the soil of our daily lives.

As offensive to many persons as the dirty joke at its rawest are those sadistic witticisms which have come to be known as "sick." Ranging from such exchanges as

"Momma, I don't like my brother."
"Shut up and eat what I give you."

to quips that wring a laugh out of visions of an atomic war, these jests make fun of grotesque events and possibilities. Yet we chuckle when we hear them. Though they deal with nothing rosier than death, pain, cruelty, deformity, disease, and disaster, they strike a note of levity in our hearts, compelling laughter often against our will.

"Mrs. Jones, your little girl has been run over by a steamroller."
"Well, I'm taking a bath now. Just slip her under the door."

"Mrs. Smith, can Bobby come out and play baseball?"
"But you know he has no arms or legs."
"That's all right. We only want him to be second base."

The listener may be shocked, he may wince, but as often as not he chortles too, and goes on to retell the joke at the next opportunity. How can we explain it? If we pursue the line of thought we have been following, we must infer that the appeal of sadistic humor discloses a fund of viciousness (or, at the very least, callousness) within us. We like being freed from our ethical outlooks in which only pleasant, compassionate emotions can be enjoyed, for secretly a segment of us gloats at the spectacle of human suffering.

It may be difficult to admit, but deep within us we are all insensitive to the agony of others. Our eyes may shed tears and our lips fashion phrases of condolence, but in the stillness of our hearts we do not care. Reprehensible as it seems, that is part of our truth—and a not insignificant part, as this kind of humor reveals.

Malicious laughter is common at every stage of life. Young children, for example, get a kick out of tricking people with such conundrums as the following:

Adam and Eve and Pinch-me went down to the river to bathe. Adam and Eve were drowned. Who was left? (When you answer, of course, you get pinched.)

Adolescent jokes, both verbal and practical, are frequently hostile and, whatever our age, we all enjoy the pie-in-the-face brand of slapstick, the witty insults on which many popular comics build their careers, and anecdotes like this one:

A boy asks his father to define the word exasperation. *"Well," says the father, "that's hard to do. But I'll give you a demonstration of its meaning, if you like."*

The boy agrees and his father instructs him to listen in on their extension phone. Then he dials a number at random. A man at the other end answers, "Hello."

"Hello," says the boy's father cheerily. "May I speak to Mr. Rutherford?"

"I'm sorry," comes the reply. "You have the wrong number."

At that he hangs up, but immediately dials again. Once more the man answers, "Hello."

Just as cheerfully, the father says, "May I speak to Mr. Rutherford, please?"

"I said," the gentleman at the other end enunciates, "you have the wrong number."

So he hangs up and dials again. "Hel-lo," comes the wary response.

"May I speak to Mr. Rutherford?"

"Dammit, I told you you have the wrong number!"

"Daddy, Daddy!" exclaims the boy. "Is that exasperation?"

"No, son. That's just irritation. Have patience." And he dials again.

"Hello!" The man's voice is trembling with indignation.

"May I speak to Mr. Rutherford, please?"

"You stupid idiot! You have the WRONG NUMBER!!"

"Daddy, Daddy, is that exasperation?"

"Not quite, my boy. I would call that aggravation. But listen closely now—here comes exasperation." And yet again he dials the well-worn digits.

"Hello," chokes the voice on the other end, almost inaudible with rage.

"Hello," chirps the father, bright as ever. "This is Rutherford calling. Any messages?"

The fact that we chuckle at scenes like this must convince us, if we need convincing, that even mature adults can respond with enthusiasm to the discomfiture of total strangers. We appreciate—let us not mince words—we *love* the misfortunes of others. There are limits, of course, to what we consider fun; if the sadistic element is cruder than our taste can tolerate, we begin to label the humor as "sick" and deny the savage joy it engenders. But within our limits and often despite them, we are frequently delighted by malicious and morbid jests.

Contrary to popular opinion, such humor is not germane to our time alone. It has existed through the ages. Trickster, in one episode of the Winnebago legend, starves some children to death while, in another, he devours his own intestines. *Galgenhumor* (gallows humor) has flourished in Europe for centuries and in this country, forty or fifty years ago, "little Willy" verses were the rage. For example:

Little Willy hung his sister,
She was dead before we missed her;
Willy's always up to tricks—
Ain't he cute? He's only six!

Willy poisoned father's tea,
Father died in agony;
Mother came and looked quite vexed—
"Really, Will!" she said. "What next?"

It is true, however, that there has been a proliferation of such wit in the last decade. Related to the blossoming of the "theater of the absurd," expanded to the proportions of a feature movie in *Dr. Strangelove* and, more recently, in *M*A*S*H*, this upsurge of laughter at horror appears to represent an attempt to cope with the anxieties of our nuclear age. Viewed in this light, our potential for callousness is not without merit. When leaders of nations can calmly consider the effects of a hundred-megaton blast on a city like New York or Moscow, we must either shriek at the monstrosity that passes for reason or find other kinds of self-protective response. Sick humor, comedies of despair, and cynical wit in general afford us some temporary, partial relief. In envisioning the worst and laughing at it, we mentally transcend the dreadful probability of our destruction.

Since death is everywhere the end of man and since, long before our physical demise, the death of our fond hopes is our inevitable share, bitter laughter seems a fitting antidote to feed on. If it is, in the largest sense, a self-preservative maneuver, an attempt to maintain integrity in the face of defeat, should we not allow ourselves that much? When the defeat is due to natural causes, few will cavil. When a man can laugh about his old age or the encroachment of an incurable disease, we will all commend him. When, however, the destruction to be faced is determined not by inscrutable fate but by the all-too-scrutable vanity, stupidity, and greed of men in power, we may doubt that the response of cynical merriment is really admirable. Since laughing helps us accept the inevitable and thus short-circuits our incentive to protest, we may question whether the humorous reaction contributes more to our salvation or to our undoing.

This is probably the strongest argument against sick humor, especially when it concerns itself with the peril of nuclear war. Movies like *M*A*S*H* and *Dr. Strangelove*, in this view, undermine our mental bulwark against international conflict by portraying it as more ludicrous than ghastly. Besides that, the opponents of sadistic wit aver, death, pain, and destruction are just not laughable phenomena; considering their dreadful nature, only shallow or morbid individuals can care to joke about them.

While this outlook contains a measure of truth, it fails to penetrate the crux of the matter. Laughter, in its essence, is not nice; it is not practical; it is not reasonable; it is not mature. Nor is it necessarily un-nice, impractical, unreasonable, or immature. It spans these categories. We must comprehend it as an instinctive, self-protective, homeostatic response—a natural avenue for reducing tension, shaking off anxiety, overcoming stagnation, and transcending all our mortal bonds. As such, it knows no ethical barriers, no holy ground. Half a century ago, one of Sholom Aleichem's characters wrote to his friend in America:

"Dear Yankel, you ask me to write you at length, and I'd like to oblige, but there's really nothing to write about. The rich are still rich, and the poor are dying of hunger, as they always do. What's news about that? And as far as the pogroms are concerned, thank God we have nothing more to fear, as we've already had ours—two of them, in fact, and a third wouldn't be worthwhile . . . All our family got through it safely, except for Lippi, who was killed with his two sons . . . Oh yes, and except Hersh. Perel was found dead in the cellar, together with the baby at her breast. But as Getzi used to say: 'It might have been worse . . .' You ask about Heshel. He's been out of work now for over half a year. The fact is they won't let him work in prison . . . They're arranging great things for him, I hear: the rope, or a firing squad. It's all a matter of luck . . . Mendel did a clever thing, though; he up and died. Some say of hunger, others of consumption. Personally, I think he died of both. I really don't know what else there is to write about, except the cholera, which is going great guns . . ."

The blithe indifference he displays is not far removed from callousness. It is saved from viciousness by the fact that the writer himself has participated in the horror he is describing —a fact which, of course, makes all the difference in the world—but the point is that, as a general attitude, it helps us cope with distress by portraying the most heartrending tragedies as merely scenes in the eternal human comedy.

Viciousness, callousness, indifference: these are the qualities we must play host to if we are to let this stream of humor flow through our veins. Like blatant sexuality, they flourish in the absence of love. In the last analysis, lust and viciousness are twins born to the self-centeredness that characterizes our being before we become capable of compassion. Immoral humor demonstrates that this self-centeredness never dies but in fact remains an integral part of our vitality throughout our lives.

Here again we come upon the core of paradox out of which humor grows. Without love and compassion we are less than human, yet love and compassion are burdens from which we crave respite. Consideration for the suffering of others puts a drain on our tranquility; anxiety concerning our own welfare adds a further load. If, in defense, we mock it all, we allow ourselves to go on living happily despite the specters that loom around us. The spirit of humor demands that we acknowledge, in spite of our need for love, our undeniable lust, and in spite of our capacity for caring, our inclination to not give a good goddamn.

We are reluctant to make these acknowledgments because they clash with our image of ourselves as good people. A good person, we rightly believe, is characterized by unselfishness, concern for others, and a real ability to love. Humor, however, is not allied to goodness; it is allied to nature and to wholeness. To allow our sense of humor its full development, we must be willing to shift our primary aim from the attempt to be good to the attempt to be natural. Only as the latter goal takes precedence in our value system can we swim with the humorous stream in its darkest, most disturbing currents.

Freedom
from
Reason

"You are old, Father William, the young man said,
And your hair has become very white;
And yet you incessantly stand on your head—
Do you think, at your age, it is right?

In my youth, Father William replied to his son,
I feared it might injure the brain;
But now that I'm perfectly sure I have none,
Why, I do it again and again."*

Q: Why do elephants need trunks?
A: They have no glove compartments.

Q: What did the banana say to the elephant?
A: Nothing. Bananas don't talk.

From *Alice in Wonderland* to the recent spate of elephant
conundrums, nonsense provides a source of mild amusement

---

* Lewis Carroll, *Alice in Wonderland.*

for all. Because of its playful character, it is deemed more appropriate for children than adults, but the truth is that everyone can enjoy it. In all known cultures (excepting, of course, the Zombrian*) and at all times and non-times too, young and old alike have frolicked in its refreshing waters.

Why do we find it pleasant? What exactly does it do for us? Before we begin to answer, let us examine another member of the species:

* A pre-Prestidigian offshoot of the ancient Itchikitchi cult.

What does it have in common with Father William and the elephant jokes? Clearly, they all represent absurdities. A hobbyhorse in a horse race, an old man minus his brain, a talking banana, and an elephant constructed like a car: each of them dispenses with reason. By inviting us to contemplate incredible events, they spring us free from rationality, from the monotony of humdrum sensible thought.

Nonsense, we may say, supplies a recess from reason; that's why we enjoy it. Well and good. I have no argument with this observation, as far as it goes. If, however, we are to probe the subtler workings of our subject, we must peer a little deeper. When we do, we will find that both the cartoon and the quips—all of nonsense, in fact—do not break us free from logic in just any way at all, but they do so in a very special manner: they almost make good sense.

Look back, as though with fresh eyes, at our sketch. At first glance, the scene seems believable; then, within an instant, its absurdity registers. It does not present a chaotic scrawl, but a seemingly coherent picture that turns out to be impossible. The effect achieved is a trick on our common sense. The same is true of *Alice in Wonderland*, of the elephant jokes, and even of so childish a riddle as:

Q: What is black and white and red all over?
A: A blushing zebra.

In each case we are led to feel that something sensible is being presented, then suddenly we see instead an absurd image.

A related method of achieving this effect is illustrated in the following story:

A man brought his dog into a bar and ordered two martinis, one for each of them. The bartender served them without hesitation, and they drank their drinks and left. The same procedure was repeated day after day. One afternoon, however, the dog appeared by himself. Still without question the bartender served him. The next day the man arrived and thanked the bartender. "That was very nice of you," he said, "and I have brought you a little present to express my appreciation." Whereupon he produced a large red lobster. "Thanks," said the bartender. "I'll take him home for dinner." "Oh no," replied the customer. "He's already had his dinner. Why don't you take him out to a movie instead?"

Having accepted an improbable premise, we are led to a ridiculous conclusion—but there is an intrinsic logic to it all. If we can have a dog drinking martinis, why not a lobster going to the movies? We have been induced to participate in a coherent sequence of mounting absurdity; the manner of reason itself has been used to evoke the nonsensical.

A neater example, perhaps, is the joke about the man in the butcher shop:

"I'll have a pound of kidlies, please," he said.
"You mean kidneys, don't you?" the butcher asked.
"I said kidlies, didl I?" the customer replied.

Here the logical consistency of the absurdity is obvious, and it is precisely that which lends charm to the story.

Also to the point is the vaudeville dialogue:

"Didn't we meet in Chicago?"
"No, I've never been to Chicago."
"Neither have I. It must have been two other fellows."

In all these witticisms, the spark of laughter is ignited not by a crude disregard for logic but by a twisting of logic into foolishness. Most nonsense, we must understand, does not evade the intellect; it confounds it. And the finest nonsense, we must recognize, is created not by morons but by highly logical minds.

> *"Which reminds me," the White Queen said, looking down and nervously clasping and unclasping her hands, "we had such a thunderstorm last Tuesday—I mean one of the last set of Tuesdays, you know."*
>
> *Alice was puzzled. "In our country," she remarked, "there's only one day at a time."*
>
> *The Red Queen said, "That's a poor thin way of doing things. Now here we mostly have days and nights two or three at a time, and sometimes in the winter we take as many as five nights together—for warmth, you know."*
>
> *"Are five nights warmer than one night, then?" Alice ventured to ask.*
>
> *"Five times as warm, of course."*
>
> *"But they should be five times as cold, by the same rule."*
>
> *"Just so!" cried the Red Queen. "Five times as warm, and five times as cold."**

The impeccable construction of this bit of foolery reveals a keen mentality toying with the basic categories of rationality, turning time itself on its head to see how the world might look if its fundamental qualities were different. Repeatedly, in Lewis Carroll's work—as in the work of all the best nonsense humorists—we are witness to the drama of reason undoing its own principles, leaping over its own fences to gambol in the fields it itself has outlawed.

What can we make of it all? What can we say of the fact

---

* Lewis Carroll, *Alice in Wonderland.*

that the absurd always has had a widespread popular appeal? And what can we infer from the observation that the finest nonsense does not break away from common sense in the careening vehicle of chaos but takes us on an excursion into absurdity riding the rails of reason itself?

As human beings we are capable of visualizing things which cannot be, conjuring up both frightening and wondrous fantasies, dispensing with the boundaries of time and space, the law of cause and effect. There is a wealth of irrationality in us. It may be the source of much anguish, yet it also furnishes the most ecstatic joys we know. As anyone recalling youthful dreams of glory can attest and as the state of romantic infatuation proves, an irrational distortion of reality is a potent formula for bliss. Our reasoning abilities, however, act to tone it all down: to modify, control, and stabilize our moods and fantasies. While logic, therefore, may alleviate distress, it also curtails and inhibits joy. Much as we can profit from thinking things through, we must admit that reason is an agent of constriction over the free and glorious play of the mind.

Our delight in nonsense humor reflects the extent of our drive to break loose, to shake off the bonds of sensibleness and frolic in the novelty of free-associative thinking. It shows us, if we did not know it otherwise, that there is in each of us an ever-present readiness to dislodge the burden of common sense that keeps us plodding our weary way. It illuminates, too, the reason why both children and mentally unstable persons know the taste of delight more intimately than the ordinary adult citizen; whatever they may lack in judgment, they are more capable, more ready, to slip loose of reality and let their minds leap about.

Shall we, then, strive to become insane, regress to infancy, or in some fashion manage to be done with reason? Is that what it takes to develop our sense of humor in this direction? No; not at all. Effective absurdity, as we have seen, does not result from gibberish.* On the contrary, it employs the faculty of logic itself to produce illogic. Think back to the illustrations we have examined or consider this classic definition:

A specialist is an expert who learns more and more about less and less until in the end he knows everything about nothing.

It is witty because (quite apart from our envy of specialists and the retribution we gain in spelling them off) we detect a marvelous beauty in this image of perfection improving itself until it achieves an apotheosis of nullification.

We must concede that many people—all children, surely, and possibly most adults—on reading Alice's adventures or hearing nonsense quips, enjoy them simply as an escape from reason and fail to appreciate their intrinsic logic. Nevertheless, the logical roots are there and demand attention in any thorough discussion. What they suggest, in sum, is the exciting proposition that, while a recess from reason gives pleasure to everyone who has felt the compulsion to make

---

* It may appear to settle there in the famous stanza,
> *'Twas brillig and the slithy toves*
> *Did gyre and gimble in the wabe:*
> *All mimsy were the borogoves,*
> *And the mome raths outgrabe.*

but careful consideration should make it clear that even this poem's appeal lies in its tantalizing approximation to sensible poetry—in particular, to the onomatopoeic exuberances of the Romantics.

sense most of the time, it is most distinctly liberating to the intellectual, for it meets a need that is paramount in him: the need to fly free of his obsessive logic and refresh in himself the awareness that all his serious thought leads nowhere in the end.

But why call that awareness liberating? Is it not a depressing, even devastating, insight? After all, the notion that one's most developed faculty is in the long run fruitless undercuts the solidity of one's whole orientation. If I, as an intellectual, admit that intellectual pursuits are ridiculous, what have I left to cling to? With what shall I justify my existence?

Hopefully, nothing. Yes, nothing. That is the whole point. That is the liberation laughter strives toward: a state of mind keenly aware of its contingency, its relativity, its fallibility. The insight that is devastating to my identity as an intellectual is liberating to my identity as a human being. In running my reasoning faculties into a blind alley or sending them off to chase their tails, I free myself from reliance on them; in laughing at their discomfiture, I assert my independence from them.

The standpoint nonsense validates is not anti-intellectual; it is post-intellectual. As the element of nonconformity in humor demands that we become elastic with regard to our inclinations to conform, the element of illogic demands that we become elastic regarding our inclinations to make sense. Our sense of humor, it suggests, can be cultivated by the exercise of challenging the tyranny of reason. That goes for everyone—but for the intellectual in particular, the experience of reason confounding itself is possibly the greatest boon the ludicrous provides. Ironic it may be, but like the Zen *koans* which offer enlightenment through mystification, nonsense—a trivial, frivolous, childish form of wit—brings freedom and renewed vitality to the most mature, developed minds.

"Lest ye become as little children," Jesus warned, "ye shall not enter into the Kingdom of Heaven." These hallowed phrases seem a far cry from "'Twas brillig and the slithy toves . . . ," but in point of fact they lead us to the same elusive goal. The peculiar pleasure we derive from nonsense indicates that, having amassed experience, we crave to recapture innocence and, having fed on knowledge, we thirst for a refreshing sip of the absurd.

Freedom
from
Language

Puns have been called the weakest form of wit. They rarely elicit a peal of laughter, but are greeted with a groan or, at best, a grin. We accord them, nevertheless, a place in the household of humor, for they share a common heritage with their more illustrious relatives. Consider these hoary examples:

No gnus is good gnus.

Knock knock.
Who's there?
Ostrich.
Ostrich who?
Ostrich in time saves nine.

Did you hear what happened when the butcher's wife backed into the meat slicer? Disaster!

What is actually occurring here? In each instance, a familiar word acquires increased meaning. Instead of being confined to its usual connotations, it is made to suggest two
different things at the same time.

Why is this amusing? Unbeknownst to our conscious judgment, it seems, we experience our language as a restrictive
mode of expression. The trick of saying a new thought with
old words, or a double thought with a single word, affords us
a sense of mental expansion, for adherence to correct verbal
usage inhibits the natural play of our minds.

At first blush, this may seem a doubtful thesis. Verbalization, after all, is our central means of communication. While
we express ourselves, to some extent, through gestures and
grimaces, the bulk of our thoughts must be clothed in words
to get across to other individuals or even to lodge clearly in
our own minds.

That much may be so, and yet there is evidence that language restrains us, too. At times we feel compelled to borrow
phrases from another tongue, a virtual admission that our
own verbal system fails to express all the nuances of our
thought. More often we refrain from saying anything at all,
because we know no terms for the complexities and subtle-
ties we register. And even when we do speak out, the requirements of proper speech inhibit the flow of our minds. A
grammatically correct phrase makes one point at a time; it
does not say several unrelated things simultaneously. But we
experience unrelated things simultaneously. As I write this
paragraph, for instance, I am aware of the hum of the air-
conditioning unit in my office, the feel of my clothing
against my skin, the taste of the orange I have just eaten, my

mingled satisfaction and dismay over the progress of this chapter, and a host of other personal concerns. Were I to try to convey it all linguistically, however, I would be hard put to reproduce it in a form approximating the simultaneity of my experience.

Many modern writers, endeavoring to render mental states more adequately, have dispensed with the limitations of conventional language. The uncapitalized, unpunctuated poetry of e e cummings and James Joyce's experiments in the novel both bank heavily on breaking through the barriers of familiar typography and grammar. So doing, they achieve a remarkable widening of mental horizons. Take, as an illustration, Joyce's title for his final work: *Finnegans Wake*. The phrase, employed as a double play on words (Finnegan as a man's name and Finn-again; wake as a deathwatch and an arising), conveys to the initiated several layers of meaning. Finn was a legendary Irish hero, thus a national figure; Finnegan was a hod-carrier who was killed in a fall but later arose at his own wake and joined the merriment. The book, by implication, deals with the theme of death and resurrection, with the fall of man and his rebirth, as this event occurs both in individual lives and in the lives of nations. Through a distillation of associations, the complex object of the book is set forth in its deceptively simple title.

While Joyce's *tour de force* seems far removed from the silliness of puns, identical factors are involved. A foolish quip like "No gnus is good gnus" may not be profound, but it too distills associations to produce an unusual line of thought. Punning at any level excites expanded ideation, a creative escape from the inhibiting rigors of words.

If this is really the case, why are puns such a weak form of humor? The answer lies in the nature of language, as we have already discussed it. Plays on words are rarely very funny, because the restrictions imposed by words are rarely very frustrating. While it is true, as we have seen, that some mental operations cannot be expressed by following the rules of ordinary language, most of us suffer only minor inconvenience as a consequence. Inveterate punsters tend to be highly literate people: teachers, writers, and other intellectuals who frequently resort to words to communicate their subtlest thoughts. One needs to be immersed in verbalization to feel free to pun with impunity.

Up to this point we have been concentrating on the form or mechanics of punning, on the fact that it releases us from the customary limits of linguistics and packs two unrelated thoughts into one simple word or phrase. The content of puns, however, demands our attention too. It ranges from pointless to meaningful, and our reactions depend in part on this very quality.

The ability to take one's humor neat—to enjoy it fully without additional gratification—may mark the true *aficionado*, but, unpolished as most of us are, we need to have other appetites whetted before we respond with gusto. Once we have reached adulthood, we labor under so many kinds of inhibitions that a joke that releases us from grammar alone cannot give us half the kick we get out of one that releases our erotic or aggressive drives as well. The riddle, "What weighs a ton and has a stick through its middle?" "A hippopopsicle" is certainly delightful. Yet it fails to deliver the abiding satisfaction Democrats enjoyed when some of them attached to Barry Goldwater's billboard sign, "In your heart you know he's right," the rejoinder, "Yes—extremely right." Similarly, the pun about the butcher's wife ("Disaster!") amuses us as much with its erotic titillation as with its verbal ingenuity.

The pleasure we derive from puns is compounded by the connotations of the newly created expression. It is founded, nevertheless, on the fundamental enterprise itself: the twisting of words to convey unexpected thought. Trite as the products may be, the exercise amounts to a rudimentary creative process, for it involves nascent ideation—new images and ideas being formed out of old dull parts.

On the basis of these observations, what can we conclude? To cultivate our sense of humor further, we must become prestidigitators of words. It is not a matter of abandoning verbal fluency and regression into imprecision; quite the contrary—the task is one of becoming master of language instead of its servant. It requires the ability to register the meaning of what is being said, yet not get stuck in it, to see a word as it is and at the same time see what it resembles, what it could— with a little help—become. It calls for a nimble tongue and an equally nimble mind. It calls, in the last analysis, for a mental condition that apprehends language less as a vehicle of truth than as a plaything of the spirit.

"Ladles and jellybeans," child orators proclaim, "pull up your sheets and lend us your rears." The more we can enjoy and produce that kind of frivolity, the closer we come to the ground in which humor thrives. Our employment of words is closely related to our employment of thoughts. The former, in fact—as semanticists have shown—often limits and distorts the latter. By remaining within the confines of our language system, we restrict the possibilities of our experience. Punning itself does not, of course, produce new vistas of thought. In encouraging us to fool around with our verbalizations, however, it lubricates the cogs of our mentality.

Freedom
from
Naiveté

Compared to the clarity of which we are capable, most of us live most of the time in a mental fog. Like children in a world too frightening to face, we float in a haze of half-baked notions, roseate illusions, and oversimplifications. The facts of life are either too ugly or too confusing for us to accept, so we avert our eyes whenever possible. As a consequence, we conduct our lives half-blind, short-sighted in our understanding of the world and of ourselves as well.

Whatever powers of comprehension we possess, it is a sad but indisputable fact that we empioy them only fragmentarily. To see things clearly, as they are, appears to tax our will. We resist it stubbornly—and yet we are capable of doing it. We are capable of rising above our pedestrian levels of thought and generating lucid insights into the ways of mankind. We are capable of unearthing buried truths about ourselves, and we are capable, at our best, of grasping the grotesque absurdity and pathos of the human scene.

Humor, at *its* best, encourages such a grasp. When comic sequence is transmuted into art, we are led to look into the heart of humanity, to acknowledge both our pitiful and our admirable traits and to appreciate their constant intermixture. Humorists of the highest caliber do more than make us laugh; they make us see. They free us from our normal, everyday naiveté and provoke us to perceive life as it is beneath the veils of simplemindedness and pretense.

In the early 1900s, Finley Peter Dunne, in the guise of an Irish bartender known as Mr. Dooley, furnished many such perceptions. Commenting on the possibility of an international police force designed to keep imperialistic powers in line, Mr. Dooley once opined:

"Be hivins, Hinnissy, I looked forward to th' day whin, if a king, impror, or czar started a rough-house, th' blue bus wud come clangin' through th' sthreets an' they'd be hauled off to Holland f'r trile. . . . I thought th' coort wud have a kind iv a bridewell built, where they'd sind th' internaytional dhrunks an' disordhlies, an' where ye cud go anny day an' see Willum Hohenzollern cooperin' a bar'l, an' me frind Joe Chamberlain peggin' shoes. . . . But it hasn't come. . . . I want to see th' day whin just as Bill Hohenzollern an' Edward [of England] meets on th' corner an' prepares a raid on a laundhry a big polisman will step out iv a dure an' say: 'I want ye, Bill, an' ye might as well come along quiet.' But I suppose it wud be just th' same as it is now in rale life."
"How's that?" asked Mr. Hennessy.
"All th' biggest crooks wud get on th' polis foorce," said Mr. Dooley.

Speculating on his own death, Mr. Dooley observed:

"I'm dead, mind ye, but I can hear a whisper in th' furthest corner iv th' room. Ivry wan is askin' ivry wan else why did I die. 'It's a gr-reat

loss to th' counthry,' says Hogan. 'It is,' says Donahue. 'He was a fine man,' says Clancy. 'As honest a man as iver dhrew th' breath iv life,' says Schwartzmeister. 'I hope he forgives us all th' harm we attempted to do him,' says Donahue. 'I'd give annything to have him back,' says Clancy. 'He was this and that, th' life iv th' party, th' sowl iv honor, th' frind iv th' disthressed, th' boolwark iv th' Constitution, a pathrite, a gintleman, a Christyan an' a scholard.' 'An' such a roguish way with him,' says th' Widow O'Brien.

"That's what I think, but if I judged fr'm expeeryence I'd know it'd be, 'It's a nice day f'r a dhrive to th' cimitry. Did he lave much?' No man is a hero to his undhertaker."

In a famous article, "The Crusade Against Vice," he remarked:

"Vice . . . is a creature of such heejous mien, as Hogan says, that th' more ye see it th' betther ye like it."

Mr. Dooley's views were more than amusing. They were, in their homely way, enlightening, for they provided a shrewd assessment of the corruption of men in power, the callousness of so-called friends, the emptiness of pious sentiments, and the fatal attractiveness of evil.

This function of humor may seem unlike the kind of operation we have been discussing, but it belongs to the very same class of events. Naiveté and self-delusion are as inhibiting to our mental freedom as conventionality, morality, and reason. When we fail to perceive the actuality of our circumstances and allow ourselves to live in relative ignorance, we inhabit a narrower range of consciousness than we possess. When we fail to recognize the aspects of human behavior that Mr. Dooley was so adept at pointing out, we move in a restricted plane of existence. Enlightenment, it should be clear, is as liberating an experience as any we can name, and it is one of humor's functions to promote it.

Unfortunately, however, most of us are so conditioned to

the role of passive recipient of humor that, when a skillful satirist provides a shrewd assessment of life as it really is, we awaken for a moment to the revelations of his views, then sink back into the torpor of our own murky minds. Like the inhabitants of Laputa, we are content to be shaken out of our stupor every now and then, but we generally neglect to exercise the awareness of which we ourselves are capable.

We could all profit more from our exposure to professional wits and humorists if we adopted an attitude of active participation in their monologues and observations. Like the serious student of music or art in contrast to the idle listener or spectator, we must learn to pay close attention to the productions of the masters. Our own wit may spark into life without benefit of instruction, but studying the thoughts and outlooks of the finest humorists amongst us cannot help but fan the flames of our natural inclinations.

The importance of the shift from passive to active absorption can hardly be overemphasized. We may read, watch, and listen all our lives to the comic geniuses of our culture and never learn a thing to help us in our own development. If we make the shift, however, we may soon find ourselves acquiring not a repertoire of second-hand jokes, but the facility to see things clearly that characterizes the genuine satirist.

Ironically enough, the revelations of the satirist can be produced from two diametrically opposed positions. As he strips away the veils, his mood may be bitter or compassionate, his judgment cynical or benevolent. Jonathan Swift, Mark Twain in his later years, and the classical playwright Molière convey the former attitude; James Thurber, Mark Twain in his early career, and Sholom Aleichem convey the latter.

In *A Tale of a Tub*, Swift says:

> *Those entertainments and pleasures we most value in life are such as dupe and play the wag with the senses. For if we take an examination of what is generally understood by happiness, as it has respect either to the understanding or the senses, we shall find all its properties and adjuncts will herd under this short definition: that it is a perpetual possession of being well deceived.*

Precisely echoing his sentiments, Mark Twain in his declining years writes:

> *No sane man can be happy, for to him life is real, and he sees what a fearful thing it is.* *

Twain's cynicism is expressed in all his later works—most succinctly, perhaps, in "The Five Boons of Life":

I

In the morning of life came the good fairy with her basket, and said: "Here are gifts. Take one, leave the others. And be wary, choose wisely! Oh, choose wisely! for only one of them is valuable."

The gifts were five: Fame, Love, Riches, Pleasure, Death. The youth said eagerly:

"There is no need to consider": and he chose Pleasure.

He went out into the world and sought out the pleasures that youth delights in. But each in its turn was short-lived and disappointing, vain and empty; and each, departing, mocked him. In the end he said: "Those years I have wasted. If I could but choose again, I would choose wisely."

II

The fairy appeared, and said:

"Four of the gifts remain. Choose once more; and oh remember—time is flying, and only one of them is precious."

The man considered long, then chose Love; and did not mark the tears that rose in the fairy's eyes.

After many, many years the man sat by a coffin, in an empty home. And he communed with himself, saying: "One by one they have gone away and left me; and now she lies here, the dearest and the last.

---

* Mark Twain, *The Mysterious Stranger*.

Desolation after desolation has swept over me; for each hour of happiness the treacherous trader, Love, has sold me I have paid a thousand hours of grief. Out of my heart of hearts I curse him."

III

"Choose again." It was the fairy speaking. "The years have taught you wisdom—surely it must be so. Three gifts remain. Only one of them has any worth—remember it, and choose warily."

The man reflected long, and then chose Fame; and the fairy, sighing, went her way.

Years went by and she came again, and stood behind the man where he sat solitary in the fading day, thinking. And she knew his thought:

"My name filled the world, and its praises were on every tongue, and it seemed well with me for a little while. How little a while it was! Then came envy; then detraction; then calumny; then hate; then persecution. Then derision, which is the beginning of the end. And last of all came pity, which is the funeral of fame. Oh, the bitterness and misery of renown! Target for mud in its prime, for contempt and compassion in its decay."

IV

"Choose yet again." It was the fairy's voice. "Two gifts remain. And do not despair. In the beginning there was but one that was precious, and it is still here."

"Wealth—which is power! How blind I was!" said the man. "Now, at last, life will be worth the living. I will spend, squander, dazzle. These mockers and despisers will crawl in the dirt before me, and I will feed my hungry heart with their envy. I will have all luxuries, all joys, all enchantments of the spirit, all contentments of the body that man holds dear. I will buy, buy, buy! deference, respect, esteem, worship— every pinchbeck grace of life the market of a trivial world can furnish forth. I have lost much time, and chosen badly heretofore, but let that pass; I was ignorant then, and could but take for best what seemed so."

Three short years went by, and a day came when the man sat shivering in a mean garret; and he was gaunt and wan and hollow-eyed, and clothed in rags; and he was gnawing a dry crust and mumbling:

"Curse all the world's gifts, for mockeries and gilded lies! And miscalled, every one. They are not gifts but merely lendings. Pleasure, Love, Fame, Riches, they are but temporary disguises for lasting realities—Pain, Grief, Shame, Poverty. The fairy said true: in all her store

there was but one gift which was precious, only one that was not valueless. How poor and cheap and mean I know those others now to be, compared with that inestimable one, that dear and sweet and kindly one, that steeps in dreamless and enduring sleep the pains that persecute the body, and the shames and griefs that eat the mind and heart. Bring it! I am weary, I would rest."

V

The fairy came, bringing again four of the gifts, but Death was wanting. She said:

"I gave it to a mother's pet, a little child. It was ignorant, but trusted me, asking me to choose for it. You did not ask me to choose."

"Oh, miserable me! What is there left for me?"

"What not even you have deserved: the wanton insult of Old Age."

The tone of the piece is morbid, but its truth is timeless. Satire at its most acerbic, it forces us to face a series of unpleasant facts of life. We may not laugh or even smile, but in the recesses of our minds we know that we are witnessing the ironic shoals on which our own aspirations, too, must eventually founder.

In a similar vein, Molière's *Tartuffe* exposes the crass deceit and foolish gullibility that frequently characterize human relationships. Tartuffe, the pious hypocrite, succeeds in winning the admiration of his benefactor, M. Orgon:

ORGON: *Oh! Had you seen him as I first saw him, you would have the same affection for him that I have. Every day he would come to church and with a gentle expression kneel down in front of me. He attracted the attention of the whole congregation by the fervor of his prayers to heaven. He sighed in saintly rapture and kissed the ground humbly every moment, and when I came out he would come to the door to offer me holy water. Having learned who he was and that he was poor . . . I gave him presents but he always wished to return some part of them. "It is too much, too much by half," he would say. "I do not deserve your pity." And when I refused to take it back he distrib-*

uted it to the poor. At last heaven moved me to take him into my house and since then everything has seemed to prosper here. He criticizes everything and, aware of my honor, shows an extreme interest in my wife.

Only after the scoundrel has accepted betrothal to Orgon's unwilling daughter and attempts to seduce his wife in the bargain does the misguided benefactor see the light. Hiding under a table in his wife's boudoir, he hears Tartuffe say:

TARTUFFE: If heaven is the only thing which opposes my wishes I can take care of it; it need not put any restraint on your love.
WIFE: But the judgments of heaven are frightening.
TARTUFFE: I can dispel these absurd fears, Madame, for I know the art of removing scruples. Heaven, it is true, forbids certain gratifications, but there are ways of getting away with it. . . . I can initiate you into these secrets, Madame; you have only to allow yourself to be led. Satisfy my desire, and do not be afraid. I will take the sin upon myself. . . . The scandal of the world is what makes the offense, and to sin in secret is not to sin at all. . . .
WIFE: Open the door a little and look if my husband is in the passageway.
TARTUFFE: Why trouble yourself about him? Between us, he is a man to be led by the nose.

Though he is discovered and brought to justice, Tartuffe neither mends his ways nor repents his sins. He remains a hypocrite to the bitter end, and we, the audience, are made to feel contempt, not compassion, for his plight. In Molière's hero, we see a caricature of our own deceitfulness, our own propensity to exploit other people's trust and take what we can by fair means or foul. To the extent that we look down on him, we may feel uplifted in our higher moral standards. To the extent that we identify with him, however, *Tartuffe* must leave us as uneasy as a confession to an unsympathetic listener.

Recall, in comparison, James Thurber's "The Secret Life of Walter Mitty." A meek, henpecked husband indulges in dreams of glory. Cowering under his wife's dominion, in his fantasy he becomes a daring aviator, a gifted surgeon, an unequaled marksman, an unruffled court defendant, and a man's man, fearless in the face of death itself.

Something struck his shoulder. "I've been looking all over this hotel for you," said Mrs. Mitty. "Why do you have to hide in this old chair? How do you expect me to find you?" "Things close in," said Walter Mitty vaguely. "What?" Mrs. Mitty said. "Did you get the what's-its-name? The puppy biscuit? What's in the box?" "Overshoes," said Mitty. "Couldn't you have put them on in the store?" "I was thinking," said Walter Mitty. "Does it ever occur to you that I am sometimes thinking?" She looked at him. "I'm going to take your temperature when I get home," she said.

They went out through the revolving doors that made a faintly derisive whistling sound when you pushed them. It was two blocks to the parking lot. At the drug store on the corner she said, "Wait here for me. I forgot something. I won't be a minute." She was more than a minute. Walter Mitty lighted a cigarette. It began to rain, rain with sleet in it. He stood up against the wall of the drug store, smoking. . . . He put his shoulders back and his heels together. "To hell with the handkerchief," said Walter Mitty scornfully. He took one last drag on his cigarette and snapped it away. Then with that faint, fleeting smile playing about his lips, he faced the firing-squad; erect and motionless, proud and disdainful, Walter Mitty the Undefeated, inscrutable to the last.

With gentle skill the story plunges to our heart of hearts, inviting us to see and accept ourselves in the image of its hero. To see and *accept*; neither to glorify, ignore, nor disparage—but to accept. To perceive the disparity between our daydreams and the distracted, incompetent figure we cut in reality and to embrace that knowledge, to love it as Thurber loves his little, pathetic Mitty. The message is never spelled out, yet it is there as clear as day, in the author's compassionate insight. To the extent that we receive it, we are enabled to feel hopeful in the midst of hopelessness, triumphant in the face of defeat. We smile at Walter Mitty with affection, not contempt; so doing, we are encouraged to smile with affection at our own meekness and compensatory dreams of glory. We are invited, in the largest sense, to enjoy the awkward, touching creatures we can be.

Compare, in this respect, the later and the earlier Mark Twain. In *The Mysterious Stranger*, published posthumously, he declared, "It is true, that which I have revealed to you: there is no God, no universe, no human race, no earthly life, no heaven, no hell. It is all a dream—a grotesque and foolish dream. Nothing exists but you. And you are but a thought—a vagrant thought, a useless thought, a homeless thought, wandering forlorn among the empty eternities!" The cynicism of this view is absent from his major works. In Chapter 31 of *Huckleberry Finn*, for example, we find Huck wrestling with his conscience on the issue of exposing old Jim, the runaway slave who has become his friend.

It made me shiver. And I about made up my mind to pray, and see if I couldn't try to quit being the kind of a boy I was and be better. So I kneeled down. But the words wouldn't come. Why wouldn't they? It warn't no use to try and hide it from Him. Nor from me, neither. I knowed very well why they wouldn't come. It was because my heart warn't right; it was because I warn't square; it was because I was playing double. I was letting on to give up sin, but away inside of me I was holding on to the biggest one of all. I was trying to make my mouth say I would do the right thing and the clean thing, and go and write to that nigger's owner and tell where he was; but deep down in me I knowed it was a lie, and He knowed it. You can't pray a lie—I found that out.

So I was full of trouble, as full as I could be; and I says, I'll go and write the letter—and then see if I can pray. Why, it was astonishing, the way I felt as light as a feather right off, and my troubles are gone. So I got a piece of paper and a pencil, all glad and excited, and set down and wrote:

Miss Watson, Your runaway nigger Jim is down here two mile below Pikesville, and Mr. Phelps has got him and he will give him up for the reward if you send.

Huck Finn.

I felt good and all washed clean of sin for the first time I had ever felt so in my life, and I knowed I could pray now. But I didn't do it straight off, but laid the paper down and set there thinking—thinking how good it was all this happened so, and how near I come to being lost and going to hell. And went on thinking. And got to thinking over our trip down the river; and I see Jim before me all the time: in the day and in the night-time, sometimes moonlight, sometimes storms, and we a-floating along, talking and singing and laughing. But somehow I couldn't seem to strike no places to harden me against him, but only the other kind. I'd see him standing my watch on top of his'n, 'stead of calling me, so I could go on sleeping; and see him how glad he was when I come back out of the fog; and when I come to him again in the swamp, up there where the feud was; and such-like times; and would always call me honey, and pet me, and do everything he could think of for me, and how good he always was; and at last I struck the time I saved him by telling the men we had smallpox aboard, and he was so grateful, and said I was the best friend old Jim ever had in the world, and the only one he's got now; and then I happened to look around and see that paper.

It was a close place. I took it up, and held it in my hand. I was a-trembling, because I'd got to decide, forever, betwixt two things, and I knowed it. I studied a minute, sort of holding my breath, and then says to myself: "All right, then, I'll go to hell"—and tore it up.

It was awful thoughts and awful words, but they was said. And I let them stay said; and never thought no more about reforming. I shoved the whole thing out of my head, and said I would take up wickedness again, which was in my line, being brung up to it, and the other warn't. And for a starter I would go to work and steal Jim out of slavery again; and if I could think up anything worse, I would do that too; because as long as I was in; and in for good, I might as well go the whole hog.

Huck's conviction that, in following the dictates of his

heart, he is being wicked leaves us loving him all the more and through him learning the possibility of untaught goodness. Twain compels us to recognize the injustice of the law and the hypocrisy of social morality but, setting these against the innate truth and kindness of a simple boy's soul, he keeps us optimistic about our destiny.

Perhaps the most convincing exponent of compassionate irony of all is the Jewish humorist, Sholom Aleichem. His homely tales cover every aspect of Jewish life in the *shtetl** of the nineteenth century. His characters portray the fear and misery, the ignorance and poverty in which these people existed, but the life he depicts is never mean or barren. In the midst of famine and pogroms, dirt and disease, Sholom Aleichem's Jews are the richest people on earth, for they are rich in love and tradition, rich in faith and a sense of community, rich in the ability to extract the utmost pleasure from a glass of tea or a piece of herring, and rich above all in humor: in the capacity to savor their plight instead of gagging on it, to examine it with curious objectivity instead of merely crying or ranting over it.

Describing a visit he had made to Kasrilevke ("the town of the little people"), Sholom Aleichem recounts his experience in finding a hotel:

"If you'd like something cheap and classy, I'll take you to a place that'll suit you just right," my coachman suggested to me, as he drove up to a two-story building, with peeling walls bearing the large-lettered sign: "Hotel Turkalia." My cabman rapped at the door with his whip handle, shouting at the top of his voice:

"Noiach! Noiach! Where the devil are you? Open up! I've brought you a sucker."

---

* Any of the tiny East European villages in which most poor Jews lived.

The door opened, revealing a little man named Noiach, the doorman of the hotel. He grabbed my valise and without asking me any questions carried it up the stairs to the top story. Then he asked me:

"What kind of a room, by the way, would you like? With music or without music?"

"What music are you talking about?" I asked.

"I'm talking about the yactors. The yactors of the Yiddish te-ater are stopping here. And across the hall there's a cantor from Lithuania with twelve choirboys. He came here for the Sabbath services. They say he isn't a bad cantor, really a first-class cantor."

"For all I know he may be a first-class cantor. But if you'll excuse me, I'd rather have a room without music."

"As you say," Noiach the doorman answered. "I can give you another room. It's entirely up to you. But if it isn't just so, don't blame me for it."

"What do you mean 'not just so'?" I asked.

"Well," says he, "supposing you're bitten."

"Who on earth," I asked, "is going to bite me?"

"Well" he replied, "it won't be me. But there'll be those that'll bite you. We did some cleaning not long ago, just before Passover, but nothing seems to do any good, not even lamp oil."

"If that's the case," I said, "let's have the music."

Noiach the doorman showed me into a dark room, reeking of freshly tanned leather, decayed pickles, and stale cheap tobacco. Before I had time to get my bearings, Noiach seized an object and began to slap it, as you would a soft pillow to fluff it up for somebody to sleep on comfortably. While pounding away he kept on talking, apparently to himself, and raising a savage hue and cry against somebody'

"You fathead, you jobbernowl, you mooncalf! I'll give you a sock in the puss, so your crunchers will go flying! Can you beat that?—Here's everybody coming from the train, so he flops down on the bed, boots and all, sprawls out and makes himself at home. Poor delicate boy! A fine footman you are! Why the devil didn't you open the shutters or light the samovar or shine the yactors' shoes or tidy up the cantor's room? Moishe Mordkhe, get a move on! And get the hell out of here!"

Only then did I notice a tall, strapping young fellow in high boots that were oozing with grease. So that was where the smell of leather was coming from. The footman swallowed the beating the doorman gave him without a murmur, wiped his lips unconcernedly, opened the shutters, took a look at me and burst out laughing.

"Did you ever?" the doorman turned to me. "Maybe you can tell me what's so funny about it. Seems to enjoy a couple of wallops on an empty stomach. Moishe Mordkhe, get going!" he shouted. "Get the hell out of here! You lazy lout! Go on! You potato-gobbling, noodle-guzzling, doughnut-grabbing idiot! Go!"

Noiach the doorman then gave him a punch in the neck for good measure and kicked him out of the room.

"Quite a decent chap," the doorman then confided in me, "only a trifle lazy and a sound sleeper. You simply can't rouse him without a good trouncing! Poor fellow, works like a beast of burden. And everything he earns he gives to his sister. We had our hands full getting him to order a pair of boots.—And what'll you have with your tea? Some fresh baked-stuffs—egg cracknels, poppy-seed biscuits, or Kasrilevke frenzels?"

The pushy, grabby, undisciplined behavior of his fellow-men impressed him as comic, and he minced no words in saying so. His narratives, however, were never vituperative. He relished all the characters about whom he wrote, and not despite their failings but because of them. In the finest humorous vein, he saw and accepted all: never blinded himself to his people's pettiness, irritability, or prevarication, yet never let that stand in the way of his liking them.

The humorist may deride us unmercifully or, knowing all our faults, he may help us feel good to be alive. In either case, he forces us to face unpleasant facts of life. This in itself is one of humor's basic functions. In order, therefore, to cultivate our own sense of humor, we must cultivate the nerve and the astuteness to utter the unspeakable truth as we see it. To express our perception of our own and our acquaintances' ridiculousness is to allow the spirit of humor to flourish; to restrict ourselves to our social façade is to squelch it and keep it stunted.

More comprehensively, however, the satirist brings into our ken the complex ironies that underlie all human affairs. In the exercise of this ability, he attacks the single-mindedness on which our security is founded. Were we to take his message to heart, we could no longer support any cause or movement, subscribe to any political or philosophical doctrine. Neither capitalism nor socialism, black power nor white power, women's rights nor masculine ascendancy, pragmatism nor existentialism could command our allegiance, for we would know full well that all positions are biased, all arguments meretricious, all claims exaggerated. Nor could we believe in ourselves, in the sense of taking ourselves seriously, for we would be acutely aware of our fundamental ambivalence and inescapable dishonesty. Were such an awareness to dominate our consciousness, we would be free of all worldly ties. Like the Hindu in *Mukti**, we would have passed beyond the lures of reality.

It need hardly be pointed out that most of us will never attain this level of being. The gratifications of earthly life are too seductive, our need for inner harmony too insistent. We gorge ourselves on chauvinism and self-righteousness. We unify ourselves by believing in the truth or goodness of a set of values, a social program, a definable philosophy or religion, for we cannot long endure the uncertainty of utter relativity.

Yet utter relativity is humor's deepest root. If our sense of humor, therefore, is to grow to its highest reaches, we must

---

* The final stage of development, also known as *Brahman*, in which possessions, position, family ties, and even one's physical self are transcended.

let the satirical view of life flood our vision every spring. To be inundated by it is to be torn away from the mental anchors that provide our peace of mind; to be immune to it, however, is to remain a child forever. The only viable solution is to let it come and go, to absorb its implications and be freed, then to sink back into the security of narrow-mindedness. Whether the experience will, in the end, turn us into cynics or allow us to remain warmhearted is an open question; satire, we have seen, can be framed in bitterness or tolerance. One thing is certain, though. It will release us—periodically, at least—from the naiveté of single-minded views.

Freedom from Redundancy

"Are you a psychiatrist?"
"Why do you ask?"
"You're a psychiatrist."

The target of this jest embodies a debilitating condition from which we all suffer. Call it redundancy; color it any solid color; it is the condition Emerson referred to when he epigrammed, "A foolish consistency is the hobgoblin of little minds." Whether we know it or not, we are all little minds, for we all mouth habitual, automatic attitudes and conduct ourselves in mechanical, preconditioned ways.

The sketch on the following page exemplifies the condition's social spread: From the bearded hippie to the young executive, in the eyes of humor we are all automatons. We may try to escape it, to deny it, but—conservative or liberal,

intellectual or laborer—we remain unwitting prisoners to stereotyped styles of living.

The problem, to a large extent, is a result of group-identification. Most Democrats feel compelled to think like other Democrats; most Republicans to behave like other Republicans; adolescents are anxious to ape their peers, adults conform to their socio-economic class.

But it is not entirely a matter of group membership. Each and every one of us casts himself in a personal mold out of which he dares not emerge. Harry Smith incessantly acts like Harry Smith, Mary Jones is just as relentlessly Mary Jones.

Like wound-up spring-action toys, we play out our little repertoires again and again and again, for we are frightened and confused at the prospect of doing anything unlike ourselves.

The affliction is serious and all the more insidious because we fail to appreciate its effects. It keeps us from growing, from learning, and especially from understanding the validity of other people's views. We get stuck in our own identities, be they social or individual, until finally we don't see anything, say anything, or think anything except what we have seen and said and thought before.

But perhaps I am arguing the case too strenuously? Of course I am—which only illustrates the point. Whatever we do we tend to overdo, for once committed to any position we become identified with it.

There may be merit in conviction and perseverance, but the "foolish consistency" we succumb to is rooted deeper. A child of inertia and self-justification, it keeps us repeating habitual patterns long after they are out of date, and extending personal viewpoints to ridiculous extremes.

The tailor whose shop was robbed is a lighthearted case in point. Asked if he could describe his assailant, he replied, "Of course I can. He was a 38 short, let out the shoulders and take in the waist."

More biting, perhaps, are the implications of the cartoon on the following page.

It may seem merely whimsical at first glance, but if we dwell on it a moment we must recognize that in its absurdity our common foolishness is tapped. Like the unperturbed umpire, we are all bound to the conventions of our own particular games, and, even in the face of startling events, we

"Ball four!"

obsessively repeat our conditioned patterns of behavior. Inappropriate as they may be, we cannot—or will not—forgo them.

A Jewish matron runs along the seashore, screaming, "Help! Help! My son, the doctor, is drowning!" We laugh, enjoying the conceit that we ourselves are free of such stupid pride. Godfrey Cambridge proposes a Rent-a-Negro agency to supply a few selected colored people to attend white-liberal cocktail parties and give them that integrated look. We laugh again, imagining that we are free of the motives he has so slyly unearthed. But whom are we kidding? In the larger sense we are not free at all: no freer than the boastful mother, no freer than the fake white liberals. We are all hung up on some piece of self-aggrandizement, some group-sanctioned ethic, or simply some unthinking, inflexible pattern of behavior.

We do not laugh so readily at animal behavior, though it is even less flexible than our own, because we are aware that it cannot be other than it is. Controlled by its natural instincts, the savage beast is beautiful, not ridiculous. But the human beast claims reason and free will. We profess to be adaptable, intelligent creatures, capable of judgment, choice, and discretion. Perhaps the deepest irony exposed by our sense of humor is the contrast between that noble claim and the unending instances in which we behave like puppets on strings controlled by forces we deny, dancing our little jigs every day, week, and month, and changing not a bit from year to year.

Redundancy may be cast in an occupational mold: the psychiatrist forever playing psychiatrist; a national mold: the Frenchman feeling compelled to live up to his image of a

Frenchman; a religious mold: the churchgoer murmuring pious maxims; or an individual mold: you and I never deviating from our habitual attitudes and practices. As we become its victims, we degenerate into types, into robots, into integers of this or that system of living. From the proverbial Scotchman, looking to save a penny, to the professor lost in his ivory-tower speculations, every instance of people repeating themselves like broken records is a subject ripe for ridicule, for it is an example of what Henri Bergson called "the mechanical encrusted on the living."

Yet we cannot seem to stop it. No matter how ridiculous we become, we get stuck more and more in our unswerving ruts of being. Their lure, it appears, is too seductive to resist. On the one hand, repetitive patterns of behavior vastly simplify our lives. They save us the effort of continual self-assessment and decision-making. All we have to do to be content, we find, is what we've always done, or what our peers would do. On the other hand, they afford us a solid sense of self, a sense of clarity and integrity. By staying virtually the same for years on end, we come to pride ourselves on knowing our own mind, being stable, and having strength of character. These virtues, we believe, are indisputable, and in truth they are invaluable. Having achieved them, we know where we stand and we feel at one with ourselves.

Disconcerting as it may be, however, we must admit that, while they do us this world of good, they also inhibit our growth and diminish our fullness. Having settled on any outlook whatsoever, we are stubbornly resistant to opposing points of view because they threaten our serenity. Having found peace of mind, we are loath to relinquish it even if it means becoming narrow and dogmatic. So we are trapped in a predicament from which there appears to be no escape: the very qualities which establish our stability also stunt our further development.

Within this seeming paradox, humor offers us respite. To profit from its guidance, we must recognize our own redundancies. We must see where we are automatons, where we behave like a set of conditioned reflexes, and we must convince ourselves to forgo the pleasure. When we discover how we are stuck in an occupational rut, a political rut, a socioeconomic rut, or our own personality rut, we must try to step out of it and see what the world looks like from a different vantage point.

Our sense of humor suggests it; our sense of humor demands it. Be flexible, it advises. Be restless; be changeable; be various; be unpredictable. Its advice may be socially and psychologically troublesome, but humor's reach overshadows psychological and social convenience. It evokes the rhythm of the life process in its most elemental form. It does not tolerate redundancy in any human endeavor, for redundancy is the enemy of human vitality, and vitality—unvarnished and unprettified—is humor's favorite protegé.

A psychological in-joke clearly amplifies this argument. It concerns a Rogerian therapist: one, that is, who follows Carl Rogers' dictum that the therapist must never express an opinion or judgment of his own. According to this approach, he must confine himself to reflecting, as accurately as he can, whatever the patient is feeling and seeking to express.

In this particular story, the patient begins by complaining, "I'm really feeling miserable today."

The therapist replies, "You're feeling very despondent."

"Yes," says the patient. "I hate the world and I hate myself."

"You have no love for anybody," echoes the therapist.

"I'm so completely hopeless," exclaims the patient, "that I've decided to jump out that window and end it all."

"You're feeling suicidal," the therapist agrees.

At this juncture, the patient gets up, runs over to the window, and—sure enough!—he jumps.

The therapist, unperturbed, looks out and says, "Splat!"

It is always easy to identify redundancy in another person. Those of us who ridicule the Rogerian therapist tacitly assume that we ourselves are more adaptable. But that assumption only demonstrates how deluded we can be. Other systems of psychotherapy are just as redundant, and the psychologist who adheres to no definable system is probably redundant too, within the context of his individual personality.

Nothing is gained by hoisting the problem off our own shoulders and foisting it onto others, for the gist of the matter is that, in one form or another, all of us are its bearers.

Nor can we ever get rid of it. Like all the other conditions from which laughter liberates us, redundancy is part and parcel of our being. We need it; we love it; we cannot eliminate it. What we can do, however, and what we need to do to allow our sense of humor its scope, is to become, now and then, unlike our usual selves: giddy if we are somber, discreet if we are rash, obnoxious if we are considerate, sentimental if we are hardhearted. The extent to which we accomplish such an occasional about-face is the extent to which we encourage our humorous development; the extent to which we resist it is the extent to which we discourage its growth.

I had the good fortune recently to attend a wedding ceremony which was held on a patio next to an outdoor pool. It was a hot summer day and the guests, in formal attire, were obviously uncomfortable. After the ceremony, while everyone was sipping champagne, I noticed some of the younger members of the congregation wistfully eyeing the pool. Then suddenly, without a word of warning, one teenage girl took off her shoes and pantyhose and—formal gown and all—went flying into the water. Cries of shock, surprise, and delight—and within a few minutes she had been joined by a flock of friends. Young men stripped down to their jockey shorts or leaped in partially clothed; young women kept something or other on and dived or jumped in too. A wave of hilarity enveloped the group, both those in the pool and those of us on the sidelines. I thought that wild, impulsive spirit was beautiful, though it would have been even more beautiful if we middle-aged onlookers had participated too. For the youngsters such a fling must be exciting, but it does not take much personal daring to engage in it. For the over-forty crowd, on the other hand, it would have been memorable because the extent of shift it would have involved from our customary behavior would have been much more substantial.

Welcome change. Leap out of your ruts. Knock Emerson's hobgoblin off your backs. That is what our sense of humor requires. As the Zen master said when his pupil asked him how to attain true wisdom, "Go fetch the tea water."

Freedom
from
Seriousness

According to Max Eastman, "Humor is play. Humor is being in fun. The first law of humor is that things can be funny only when we are in fun. There may be a serious thought or motive lurking underneath our humor. We may be only half in fun and still funny. But when we are not in fun at all, when we are in dead earnest, humor is the thing that is dead."*

Translating his position into the terms of our approach, we may say that our sense of humor springs us free from seriousness and revives that lighthearted attitude of "fooling around" we knew so well as children. It is playful rather than solemn, and even when it is in earnest it is not entirely in

---

* Max Eastman, *The Enjoyment of Laughter*, Simon and Schuster, 1936.

earnest. If a friend at whose home we are dining offers us an extra helping and we say, "No thanks, I've already had two," and he replies, "You've had three, but a fourth won't hurt," we know—or at least we hope—he is kidding. We laugh, he laughs, and no one takes offense, for the repartee has been carried out in the spirit of humor.

We need this playful attitude much more than we care to admit. The events of our lives conspire to siphon it out of us as soon as we enter adulthood. Completing our education, establishing ourselves in society, getting married and raising a family, paying our bills, becoming involved in social issues: all these actions and commitments rob us of our childish nature. We proceed into maturity, half reluctant but half proud, and settle into the responsibilities of adult behavior.

Yet something in us recalls the bliss of the carefree spirit and delights in its reawakening. If we are not too deep in our dotage, we should be able to get a kick out of such foolish spoonerisms as:

"Mardon me, padam, but this pie is occupewed. May I sew you to another sheet?"

Or:

"It will either drain or rizzle, and there will be shattered scowers in the rountain mesorts."

Even a childish limerick should be good for a chuckle or two. Try this one for size:

A gal who weighed many an ounce
Used language I will not pronounce,
When a guy, most unkind
Pulled her chair out behind
'Cause he wanted to see if she'd bounce.

The playful mood is not entirely limited to children's jokes, of course. Sophisticated wits like Ogden Nash, Richard Armour, and S. J. Perelman have created abundant streams of ingenious tomfoolery, and popular comics like Steve Allen frequently produce it too. Consider Allen's short short story, "Mythology Simplified":

Mythology Simplified

Onus, the greatest of all the gods, and his faithful spouse, Stigma, lived peacefully for many centuries high atop Mount Ipana. They had issue from time to time, and three of their sons, Virus, Peruna, and Epidermis, decided to visit the earth below to see if the maidens of Greece were as fair of face and figure as rumor would indicate. Pumice, however, the god of Finger-stain, was very jealous when he heard about their proposed jaunt, and he sent Fulcrum, the god of Balance, to harass the three on their trip to earth. Virus, learning of Pumice's treachery, enlisted the aid of Monotony, the goddess of Inertia, and when the cards were down she did not fail him. Thundering across the heavens on her mighty steed, Pantages, she attacked Pumice's stronghold, and despite the efforts of Plethora, the goddess of Oversupply, she routed the evildoer and all his forces.

Returning homeward, unfortunately, she was set upon by Thermos and Pastrami, the gods of Hot Lunch, her horse Pantages was driven off, and she was banished to the island of Hypotenuse.

When Onus learned of this his anger knew no bounds. He at once sent for Parenthesis, the goddess of Bowed-legs, and ordered her to worm her way into the confidence of Thermos and Pastrami. Parenthesis was willing enough, but first, she announced, she would like to have Onus call back from the dead her two former husbands, Papyrus, god of Race-results, and Thesis, god of Graduation.

Onus granted her request and she forthwith set off on her assignment. Hearing that she was coming, Apathy, the god of Boredom, disguised himself as her former steward Digitalis, god of Revival, and told her that Thermos and Pastrami would welcome her with open arms.

Parenthesis, falling into this trap, sent her faithful bodyguard Perimetre back home, and thus unprotected was attacked and killed. Antithesis, long-lost son of Onus, happened to be in the neighborhood at the time, however, and reported to his father what had happened. As I recall the story Onus didn't seem to care much, and that's about all there is to Greek mythology. Next time the subject comes up at a party you may conduct yourself as an authority.

Devotees of this kind of humor are numerous. Nevertheless, most adults experience only limited enjoyment of the purely playful spirit. While delightfully insouciant, it seems too light, too innocent, to deliver deep-going satisfaction, and the free-associative process on which it rides is too unbridled for most of us to emulate. We are more likely to remember and repeat humor with a point, for it appeals not only to our carefree tendencies but to our serious concerns as well.

A traveler spends an evening in a bar in a strange town. After a few drinks, he becomes expansive, uninhibited, and finally exclaims, "President Nixon is a horse's ass!" At this a burly man stalks over to him and says, "Mister, them's fightin' words 'round here." To which the traveler replies, "I'm sorry, sir. I didn't realize this was Nixon country." "It's not," grunts the burly one. "This is is horse country."

Here we have the other extreme: a joke delivered almost entirely in earnest.

The mainstream of humor, the majority of funny stories and amusing observations, is a blend of playfulness and seriousness. Our heartiest laughter is evoked when the humorous outlook is brought to bear on an area of genuine concern. I have never forgotten an experience I had on the freeways of Los Angeles several years ago. Driving them day after day, I had become accustomed to seeing bumper stickers proclaiming, AMERICANISM IS THE ONLY ISM FOR ME, and later, to one put out by some liberal organization, reading, HUMANISM IS THE ONLY ISM FOR ME. Neither of these sentiments amused me and, in the course of time, I grew sick of re-reading them. One morning, however, I was fortunate enough to pull up behind a native wit. On his bumper was a hand-lettered sticker, decked out in red, white, and blue like the others, professing NUDISM IS THE ONLY ISM FOR ME.

That simple statement is a perfect representative of humor's primary business. Attacking the bigotry of patriotism and the righteousness of altruism with a single blow, it cuts through to the meat of things, to the bare facts of life, unadorned and unsentimentalized. In its sly wink we escape, for an instant, from our sober social selves to our lewd, grinning natural selves—a welcome recess in the plodding grind of civilized behavior.

The aim of our sense of humor is not to reduce us to a childish state of mind but to enliven our adulthood with injections of our childishness. Once we have acquired the ability to take things seriously, we need to revive the ability to take them playfully. Once we have learned how to care, we have to remember how not to care.

This aim is easy to formulate, but more difficult to put into practice than we are ready to admit. I notice, for example, in writing this chapter, how little my mood coincides with what I am saying. Attempting to find phrases to promote the reawakening of the carefree spirit, I find that I am anything but carefree myself. I pace the room, gulp cups of coffee, revise and correct every page ten times over, and in general behave like the epitome of what I am arguing against.

Nor is it only this chapter in which I have been at odds with myself. Throughout this entire work I have preached the spirit of humor and practiced the spirit of seriousness. The whole conception of a book of this nature, in fact, is antithetical to its premises. Not only is it serious; it is also redundant; it attempts, successfully or not, to make sense; and, to anticipate our next chapter, it is motivated largely by egotistical needs.

My predicament, however, is representative of the predicaments we all face in attempting to cultivate our humorous faculties. If we intend to move beyond confining our laughter to specific times and places, if we intend to do more than imbibe it from the performances of professional wits and comics, if we intend to allow it to infiltrate and inform our personal lives, we will have to let two antagonistic sides of ourselves come to grips with each other. We cannot eliminate our other vital concerns but, if we really mean to cultivate our sense of humor, we cannot continue to take them as seriously as in the past.

Everything we do with utter seriousness can drive us to despair. Even such lighthearted events as parties, vacations, and making love can become a burden if we perceive them as all-important, while each and every one of them can be a joyous experience if we approach it in the spirit of fun. If we could adopt the attitude of "fooling around" not just in telling jokes but in the trying arenas of our daily lives, we would frolic through our years. Life is a game, or can be seen as one, our sense of humor tells us. If we take it that way, we may never make a million dollars, win the Nobel prize, or be elected governor, but instead of pacing we may skip, instead of shouting we may sing, and instead of an ulcer we may develop a joyful heart.

This advice sounds agreeable enough, yet we may wonder about its reach. While there are certainly some concerns we would all do well to take more lightly, other events seem poorly suited to such treatment. War, for instance, is hardly an item we can take in fun. Or is it? In response to a news item declaring that "the best hiding place in event of an atomic explosion is a frozen-food locker, where radiation will not penetrate," Richard Armour composed the following poem, included in his *Light Armour*:

> *Hiding Place*
>
> *Move over, ham*
>   *And quartered cow,*
> *My Geiger says*
>   *The time is now.*
>
> *Yes, now I lay me*
>   *Down to sleep,*
> *And if I die,*
>   *At least I'll keep.*

Consider, too, the sketch shown on page 124.

We peruse this cartoon and smile. What allows us to do it? What is the cast of mind that lets us grin at the thought of human savagery? Not an attitude of fun and games, exactly; that would be too frivolous. But not one of utter seriousness either. It is best described by a phrase we have used before: the god's-eye view—the attitude of semi-detachment, of quasi-indifference, of looking down on the affairs of men as from a height. In chuckling at the idiocy of the warlike mentality, we stand above it, acknowledge it but treat it lightly in the awareness that we are touched but not contained by it. The subject is dreadful, but our reaction is casual. We are all damn fools and will forever be, we admit. Hating, fighting, killing: that's the way of the world. So, as long as we cannot stop it, we might as well get a laugh out of it. Why not? We all may be casualties tomorrow.

In its capacity for freeing us from unremitting involvement, our sense of humor represents an enormous psychological asset. There are bound to be traumatic circumstances in

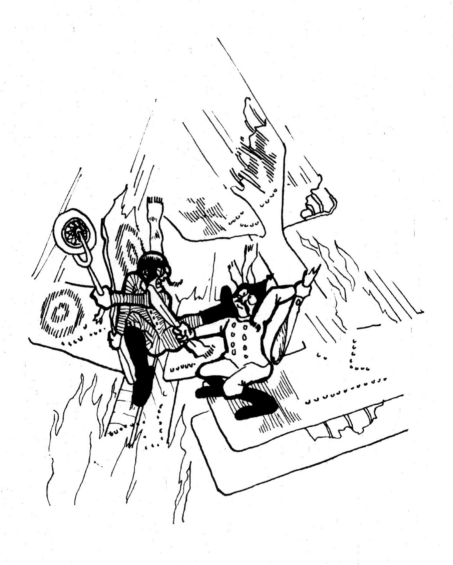

"And when we land, I'll knock your ##**!! block off!"

our lives. Whether as the victims of illness or accident, deteriorating personal relationships or collective social upheavals, we will none of us escape unhurt. In addition, we must certainly fail to achieve a good many of our heart's desires and, as if that weren't enough, our loved ones must, sooner or later, die, prove unfaithful, or wound us one way or another. Now, if when these events occur, we remain identified with our wounds, they may very well break us. But if, instead, we perceive the irony of our tragic plight, the unimportance of our downfall, the comedy of our despair, we will in that instant have risen above it. To the extent, in other words, that we can adopt a detached, playful outlook, an open-eyed but not-too-serious stance from which to observe the human scene and our own parts in it—to that extent we can become reconciled to our society, to our friends, to our families, and possibly (why not press our luck?) to ourselves.

Freedom from Egotism

Our sense of humor, we have seen, spans the most contradictory qualities we possess. It extends from nonsense to wisdom, from refinement to vulgarity, from benevolence to cynicism. Its essential dimension, however, ranges from the most degrading experience we are capable of inflicting on each other to the most beatific attitude we are capable of attaining in ourselves. It ranges from humiliation to humility.

Few human experiences are more devastating than being ridiculed. To be the butt of contemptuous wit is always a painful blow. It is designed to make us feel less than worthless, for derisive laughter suggests that we are not just deficient in some basic virtue but that our deficiency is not even worth taking seriously.

If we imagine ourselves the recipient of Dorothy Parker's observation on another woman writer—"In her latest novel, she reverts to tripe"—or Alan King's description of his doc-tor—"He specializes in eye, ear, nose, throat, and wallet"—we may approximate the feeling of being skillfully mocked. If we recall times when we made fools of ourselves in front of people we were hoping to impress, we may remember the sour taste of humiliation. In either case, we must see that coming off cheap or stupid or selfish when we are trying to look our best is guaranteed to lay us low.

It may seem like belaboring the obvious to ask why this is so, but scrutiny of well-known facts sometimes results in deepened insight. The data before us suggest that being treated as trivial or inconsequential is far more damaging to our self-esteem than any experience we can name. It appears, therefore, that above all else we need to *matter*: to be taken seriously for better or worse.

Our egos require it. Our pride, our conceit requires that other people look on us as important, that they treat us with respect. Otherwise, we are afraid we amount to nothing. But need it be so? Is it really necessary to be taken seriously to feel worthwhile? Is it not possible to accept oneself and one's life in the absence of appreciation by others?

Some people appear to have done it. They may be few and far between, but here and there a human being seems to have dispensed with pride, relinquished his ego, and attained that state of being we call humility. The attainment is so elusive, however, that it is difficult to find living persons whose characters may be taken as cases in point.

Let us turn, therefore, to literature. Dostoevsky's Alyosha Karamazov, Cervantes' Don Quixote: each embodied, in his way, a distinct strain of humility. In our own time, two famous literary figures exemplify two very different ways in which this attitude can be attained. Camus' Meursault, the hero of *The Stranger*, may be taken as an illustration of the humility of alienation; Salinger's Seymour Glass, who appears or is mentioned in several stories,* may be seen as an example of the humility of mystical communion.

Meursault, the very prototype of indifference, begins his account by reporting, "Mother died today. Or, maybe, yesterday; I can't be sure." He goes on to attend her funeral, to begin an affair with an attractive young woman, to be offered an advancement in his job, and, inadvertently perhaps, to commit a murder—but all with the same lack of emotional involvement. When his girlfriend asks him to marry her, he says he wouldn't mind; when she asks if he loves her, he replies that her question is meaningless. When he is being tried for murder, he finds it difficult to pay attention. Only at the end of his story, when a priest keeps trying to get him to pray, does he explode:

"Then, I don't know how it was, but something seemed to break inside me, and I started yelling at the top of my voice. I hurled insults at him, I told him not to waste his rotten prayers on me; it was better to burn than to disappear. . . . Actually, I was sure of myself, sure about everything, far surer than he; sure of my present life and of the death that was coming. That, no doubt, was all I had; but at least that certainty was something I could get my teeth into—just as it had got its teeth into me. . . . Nothing, nothing had the least importance, and I knew quite well why. He, too, knew why. From the dark horizon of my future a sort of slow, persistent breeze had been blowing toward me, all my life long, from the years that were to come. And on its way that breeze had leveled out all the ideas that people tried to foist on me in the equally unreal years I was then living through. What difference

---

* "A Perfect Day for Bananafish"; *Raise High the Roof Beam, Carpenters; Franny and Zooey.*

could they make to me, the deaths of others, or a mother's love, or his God; or the way a man decides to live, the fate he thinks he chooses, since one and the same fate was bound to 'choose' not only me but thousands of millions of privileged people who, like him, called themselves my brothers. . . . It was as if that great rush of anger had washed me clean, emptied me of hope, and, gazing up at the dark sky spangled with its signs and stars, for the first time, the first, I laid my heart open to the benign indifference of the universe."

In the context of the inevitability of death, Meursault suggests that it makes no difference how we live. Finding it impossible to care about the things most people think important, he exists for the moment alone. He is innocent of pride and ambition, free of hypocrisy, and blankly candid—yet he seems more a monster of detachment than a figure worthy of emulation. He embodies the humility of utter cynicism; he cannot believe in mankind or even in man's ideals, for he is allied with "the benign indifference of the universe."

Seymour Glass, in contrast, knows full well the stupidity and pettiness of human beings, but he loves them all the more because of it, and he tries (albeit unsuccessfully) to find a place for himself in this world. He too is a radical innocent, devoid of pride and ambition, but he is anything but a cynic. In *Franny and Zooey*, his sister Franny experiences a crisis because of her inability to tolerate the egotism of her contemporaries. Sick of their priggish conceit and her own as well, disgusted with her inability to refrain from trying to impress people, she suffers a nervous breakdown. After much hesitation, their brother Zooey, seeking to bring Franny out of her despair, recalls a childhood incident in which Seymour had given him a word of advice. It concerns the time when they were participants on a weekly radio program and, in particular, the time when he was contemptuous of the whole affair. The audience, the announcer, and the sponsors were all morons, as far as Zooey was concerned, and he no longer wanted to relate to them. Seymour, however, made him see that, disgusting as they might be, all the people he couldn't stand were a part of Divine Creation. Now Zooey passes this piece of advice on to Franny. And with it—with the message that every sad, sick, overstuffed human being in the world is a child of God—he finally gives her respite from her suffering. She is enabled to accept both herself and others, for she is awakened to the experience of selfless love.

It is not by accident that we can find humility of either sort more readily represented in fiction than in real life. Literary characters are frequently ideal types portraying attitudes their authors and readers may hunger for but never fully achieve. The sacrifice of ego drives, moreover, is the most esoteric goal human beings can strive for. Many people, in fact, deny its legitimacy. To identify with Franny in feeling sick of not having "the courage to be an absolute nobody" is, in their eyes, really sick. We cannot escape our egos, they believe; the only freedom we have is in how we choose to satisfy them.

Others, of course, disagree. Most mystics and religious believers, in particular, are convinced that the supreme experience a man can attain is the transcendence of his ego. To give up all claim to worldly fame, to cease the ceaseless attempt to prove his worth, to eschew the temptation to impress other people, is to them the highest of aims.

But perhaps the entire controversy boils down to a case of semantics. The relinquishing of ambition, after all, may be seen as a kind of ambition, and the attainment of humility may be the source of unending pride.

Be that as it may, our sense of humor strives toward this controversial way of being. Neither Meursault nor Seymour Glass, of course, is remotely a comic figure, but when we laugh at ourselves we approach their plane of existence. We accept, for the moment at least, the expendability of our conceit, for we are willing to recognize ourselves as ridiculous.

Most people agree that the ability to laugh at our own flaws and foolishness represents the ultimate in humor. There are different moods, however, in which such laughter can occur. When we mock ourselves in bitterness, feeling that we deserve a kick in the rear for whatever stupidity we have been guilty of, we are only indulging in self-directed humiliation. Implicit in such an attitude is the belief that we should be better than we are. When we laugh at ourselves with affection, though—as we might laugh at the antics of an infant or a puppy—we reach toward a kind of benign humility, for we perceive ourselves as silly but lovable.

> *Three Jews were about to be executed. They were lined up in front of a firing squad, and the captain addressed each in turn. "Do you want a blindfold?" he asked the first. "Okay," replied the Jew, with an air of resignation. "Do you want a blindfold?" he asked the second. "All right," came the equally resigned response. "Do you want a blindfold?" he asked the third. "No," said the man, with a show of defiance. At that, the second Jew leaned over to the third and whispered, "Take the blindfold. Don't make trouble."*

When a Jew is amused at this old story, portraying as it does the absurd lengths to which the reputed propensity of Jews for avoiding unpleasant scenes can go, he is exercising his ability to dispense with pride without rejecting himself because of his idiosyncracies.

A young priest, aflame with excitement, came running into the study of an elder colleague. "Come quick! Come quick!" he exclaimed. "To the nave. Jesus Christ Himself is at the altar!" The two priests hurried to the church and, sure enough, the Lord Himself knelt there in prayer. "What shall we do?" the younger man asked in perplexity. The elder, shielding his mouth with his fingers, whispered simply, "Look busy."

The Catholic—or better still, the priest—who enjoys this anecdote despite its chiding tone, is also exercising his ability to move beyond conceit.

Because of their contrived and impersonal nature, however, jokes fail to convey the gist of the humorous attainment of humility. That gist occurs, if at all, in spontaneous and personal experience only. Each individual alone knows if he has ever laughed at himself for being a fool, a coward, a lecher, a nut, or a pompous ass; laughed, that is, and found himself acceptable despite his failing. If he has, then he may congratulate himself on his humility and immediately destroy what he believes he has achieved.

The irreducible paradox out of which humor grows is as apparent here as elsewhere. We strive for freedom from our egos, but we can attain it only unconsciously, for the moment we become aware of the achievement we have lost it. At that moment, regardless of our intentions, we are once again the vain, self-righteous creatures we have always been.

It does not apply to present company, of course, but the sketch on the following page neatly makes the point.

What laughter at ourselves accomplishes is merely a temporary, fleeting escape from an inescapable condition of being. In dispensing with egotism, we dislodge the most constricting condition of all. We free ourselves from our righteousness, relinquish our conceit, but—except for the few of

". . . and so I say, in all humility . . ."

us who have already been sanctified—we cannot long exist without it. Throughout our lives we cling to our egos as a drowning man clings to a life preserver, for without them we are utterly at sea.

The current notion that a self-congratulatory pattern of behavior constitutes an ego-trip betrays a fuzzy perception of human dynamics. It implies that, except for those glaring exceptions, most of us are free of vanity. How naively self-righteous can we get! The labeling of someone else's exhibitionism as an ego-trip is itself a peculiarly egotistical maneuver, for it suggests that we, the observers, are humbler than the person on display. Perhaps we are, but then again, perhaps we are only afraid to compete.

In any case, our sense of humor, perverse as always, encourages us to forget our conceit although, or because, it is impossible to do. The more we are willing to try, however, the broader will our faculty for humor grow. Every time we laugh at our own stupid selves, we reinforce our feeling for the ludicrous. We reinforce and expand it in its most essential realm, for we remind ourselves that foolishness, like charity, begins at home.

Developing
a
Sense of Humor

To develop our sense of humor, we must foster the conditions conducive to its cultivation. Since it is part of our total psychic economy, its development depends on how we manage our minds in general. The closer we get to the attitudes we have discussed in the foregoing chapters, the broader will our sense of humor become. Like a living plant, it cannot be made to grow by tugging on it, but its growth can be encouraged by providing the nutrients on which it feeds.

We must, we have seen, become nonconformists. Aware of our society's, our peers', and our family's expectations, we must not allow ourselves to function as their servants. If we fit in perfectly with any group, we lop off a branch of our sense of humor. To enable it to flourish, we must remain iconoclasts at heart. *Nothing sacred*: that is the motto to which we must subscribe.

At the same time, we must look for avenues through which we can dislodge our feelings of inferiority. We must become adept in discovering the blemishes of our superiors, and we must become aware of the dubious merit of seeking superiority at all. Humor is the weapon of the underdog. It is one way in which he revives his self-esteem, and it thrives on the drive for self-assertion against overwhelming odds.

We must also modify our moral inhibitions. Unadulterated lust, we must admit, is part of our nature and deserves its place in any inventory of our being. Sex without love is what the renegade in us is after. To deny him his innings is to squelch a vital aspect of our faculty for humor. To invite him to participate in our game of living, however, is to help this faculty attain its full development.

Callous disregard for human suffering is another shameful part of our true being. It too must be acknowledged for our sense of humor to expand. If we remain relentlessly compassionate, we may rate high as beautiful souls, but the mocking imp will sulk and lose some of his bright vitality.

Our reasoning powers, meanwhile, must be shaken from their perch. We must indulge in foolishness, be willing to regress. Our childish delight in nonsense must be given free rein again, for humor responds to absurdity like a flower to the sun.

In a related vein, we must allow our minds to juggle with words, bend them this way and that, twist them out of shape and turn them over on their heads. Our sense of humor is restrained by our compulsion to speak sensibly. The greater the verbal elasticity we manage to acquire, the wider area we clear for its continued spread.

On the other hand, we must strive for sophistication.

Shrewd insight into the hypocrisy that rules the world takes humor a long way on its developmental journey. We must perceive the brutal facts behind the veils of pretense with which everyone—ourselves included—cloaks his intentions.

As if this were not enough, we must break loose from habitual behavior. We must cease being so much ourselves and engage in attempts to be different. No matter what our usual patterns of thought and feeling are, just because of their repetitiveness they stunt our humorous growth. The novel approach, on the other hand, is in itself conducive to its expansion.

We need, as well, to renew our playful spirits. To see life as a game no one ever wins, but a game we do not have to win because the fun is in the playing, is an attitude we need to cherish. Like rain on a budding bush, it promotes the blossoming of humor before our very eyes.

Finally, we must escape our inescapable conceit. We must become willing to relinquish pride and sacrifice self-righteousness. We must learn to accept ourselves as stupid, petty, vain, and greedy, not to mention irresponsible, deceitful, and ugly, if we mean to have our sense of humor reach its full-blown height.

This list of requirements, of course, is in itself ridiculous. Laughter is such a spontaneous reaction and humor such a unique frame of mind that any attempt to prescribe them is foolish to begin with. They are so important to our welfare, however, that ignoring them or simply hoping for them to occur seems equally foolish. All we can do, in this predicament, is take our choice of idiocies. Since we began this ill-fated inquiry with the former, we may as well follow it through to the bitter end.

Having reviewed the basic attitudes that encourage humor's growth, let us now attempt to penetrate its impenetrable core. If we can grasp, or even touch, its most elusive essence, we will be in a position to understand what it takes to have it reach its full development in us.

A while ago, on entering a library, I had an odd experience. My eyes scanned a shelf labeled RECENT BOOKS, but what registered in my mind was DECENT BOOKS. My brain immediately clicked through a deductive process, reasoning that the rest of the shelves must be filled with INDECENT BOOKS, and I found the thought so funny that I almost laughed out loud.

Let this incident serve as a representative of the essence we are seeking. It may not be hilarious, but in its little way it was a humorous event. What then, let us ask, were its fundamental qualities?

As I recall, I had been feeling overworked on that particular day but, driven by conscientiousness, had gone to the library to hunt up some obscure psychological references. The prospect of wading through those turgid texts depressed me, but I saw no way out. I was here, and the work had to be done. My slip-of-the-brain, however, furnished me with respite. If only things were different, it suggested. If only the shelves were filled with pornographic material—lusty novels, bawdy farces, collections of sly limericks and unprintable cartoons—what an afternoon I could have! In the context of a proper, serious situation, sex reared its gorgeous head. My sense of humor sprung me free—yet the freedom it provided came and went in less time than it takes me now to remember it.

While no single illustration can encompass all the facets of humor, this one is helpful insofar as it highlights two crucial points. It shows how the play of wit serves to liberate us from a burdensome frame of mind and—more important for our present purposes—it indicates the fleeting, transitory nature of this liberating experience.

Whenever humor lifts us out of one mode of being, it deposits us into another. The freedom it provides is temporary; its core quality is change. What it evokes is a realignment of our inner organization: a moment in which old mental connections are severed and new ones simultaneously created.

If her lips are on fire when you kiss her and she trembles when you hold her in your arms—look out, boy. She's got malaria.

In a statement like this, we are led along one line of thought, prepared for one sort of sentiment, and then presented with another. The experience is certainly liberating, but it is not, we must note, open-ended.

A Jew, visiting in Rome, is knocked down by a limousine belonging to the Pope. He claims he has been paralyzed by the accident and sues the Church for a million dollars. When the case is brought to court, he appears in a wheelchair and, despite the cross-examination of the Pope's attorneys, convinces the judge of the validity of his suit.

After he has been awarded the claim, the Pope's representatives ask him what he plans to do with the money. "Well," he says, "I'll tell you. In a few moments, my private attendant is going to wheel me out of here. He will take me to my limousine, which will drive me to the airport where my private airplane will be waiting. I will be flown directly to Lourdes. And at Lourdes, gentlemen—will you see a miracle!"

The law is traduced, yet justice, we feel, has been done. Through identification with the Jew, we enjoy a moment of release from the clutches of institutionalized morality. The court is fooled, the Church is swindled, and the little guy gets away with it. That in itself gives us pleasure, but the joke's *coup de maître* resides in the fact that the Church's own weapon is here turned against it. We are left in a mood of perfect contentment, for while the justice that prevails in the world is overturned another kind of justice is established.

Humorous release, we must conclude, is simply change of venue. Just as the ex-con, leaving his prison cell, emerges only into the wider confinement of life outside the walls, the sober citizen, having gotten the point of a jest, merely exchanges his ordinary outlook for a broader, subtler, or more novel one. Breaking loose from one set, we settle for another. That's the way it is, but the delight is in the process, in the experience of change.

That's the way it is, too, in our ordinary, everyday existence. Every settled mode of being becomes constrictive in time. Working at our regular routines, we yearn for a vacation. Let the vacation itself settle into a routine, however, and we soon feel inclined to get back in harness. Devoting our affections to our immediate family, we fall prey to a desire for a clandestine affair. Let us live the libertine life for a while, though, and the love of spouse and kiddies begins to seem more attractive. What we crave, these observations indicate, is not chaotic license but the opportunity for fresh experience.

The cultivation of our sense of humor, we may now infer, requires that we learn to thrive on change. It requires, therefore, the acquisition of a totally relativistic orientation. Neither the stolid reactionary nor the wild-eyed radical can qualify, for both rigidity and fanaticism are antithetical to its spirit. A developed sense of humor involves the ability to appreciate and depreciate every side of every standpoint, including the standpoint which appreciates and depreciates every side of every standpoint. If this quality seems paradoxical, it is not by accident, for humor is created out of the matrix of paradox that dogs our existence as human beings.

Born into a family, a community, a culture, endowed with regularly recurring needs, we cannot help but learn to control ourselves. We are taught to suppress our impulses, to conform to our surroundings, and in the doing we discover that the effort pays dividends. Every sacrifice of our instincts calls forth some reward; every advance in socialization is remunerated by the group. We come to accept routinization of our energies, for it brings us tangible achievements, wins us social acceptance, and insulates us from the chaos of unstructured being. As we mold ourselves into the roles our environment approves, however, we must limit the flow of our feelings, restrict the play of our fantasy, and compartmentalize our thoughts. We trade our authenticity for approval, our uniqueness for security. From the moment we begin to be socialized, we are thrust into paradox, for we are doomed to suffer from the attainment of the very attributes we must strive to achieve.

It was, we may speculate, in the press and pull of this predicament that human nature evolved a sense of humor as an out. In accordance with its origins, we must recognize, therefore, that our most fundamental problems are unsolvable. We might as well laugh, as has often been said, for otherwise there is nothing to do but cry.

Arising out of paradox, however, our sense of humor is something more than a sense of resignation. More than a release from inhibitions, too, it is, or can become, an attribute of affirmation, a yea-saying, an acceptance of the world with all its iniquity, the self with all its flaws.

This assertion may seem dubious, for much humor is concerned with ridiculing, not with accepting, the shortcomings of mankind. There is truth, too, in the adage that the clown is, underneath his gaiety, a man who suffers deeply from his own and others' failings. What these observations confirm, however, is only that humor frequently springs out of a bed of anger and despair. Without doubt that is so—yet humor itself constitutes an antidote. Whether born of lightheartedness or sorrow, it itself is joyous—just as a flower, whether it grows out of a field of grass or a heap of manure, radiates color and fragrance all the same.

The frame of mind associated with a chuckle, a smile, or a laugh is one of mastery, of conquering a specific threat or stress. Those topics at which we laugh most heartily are all, in some way, sources of anxiety or discomfort, but as we laugh at them our anxiety lessens, our discomfort decreases. In deriding our superiors, for example, we revitalize our dignity. They may be more powerful than us, but our wit seeks out their defects so that, in laughing them down, we build ourselves up. Even when we make fun of ourselves, we are engaged in working off anxiety and cultivating self-respect. When we joke about our looks or manners, our stupidity or cowardice, we are attempting to accept ourselves with all our faults. The moment before we laughed at it, the quality referred to may have been a source of dismay; in the act of finding it amusing, though, we detach ourselves from the problem, confess it, and demonstrate that we can take it in our stride.

To "get with" our sense of humor, then, we must learn to accept. To accept not injustice, hypocrisy, and foolishness, but life—life, which includes all these things, which is in fact pervaded by them. To accept life and to accept ourselves, not blindly and not with conceit, but with a shrug and a smile. To accept, in the end, existence, not because it's wonderful, not because it's divine, not because it's just or reasonable or even satisfactory, but simply and plainly because it's all we've got.

Section
Two

The
Creative Element

Throughout the first part of this study, we have been concerned with the content of humor to the neglect of its form or structure. We have seen how aggressiveness, sex, and other drives add zest to our smiles and laughter, but we have failed to delineate the process by which the ludicrous operates. Like painting, music, and poetry, humor occurs in sequential patterns. While these patterns are neither as subtle nor as complex as those of the arts, they are equally important to the effectiveness of even the simplest of jokes.

Q: How do porcupines make love?
A: Carefully.

ALWAYS BE SINCERE—whether you mean it or not.

What are the structural qualities of these representative

quips? Quite apart from their subject matter, how are they built or developed? Each of them, it should be apparent, suggests a mood or line of thought and then dispels it in a novel manner. When we hear the question, "How do porcupines make love?" we either anticipate some reference to actual mating habits or experience a moment of puzzlement. In any case, not knowing what to answer, we are put in a position of a person faced with the spread-out pieces of a jigsaw puzzle. When told the answer, "Carefully," we find the puzzle fitted together in a novel configuration. As we read the dictum, "Always be sincere," we experience the oppressive feeling of being moralistically advised, but as we go on to register the addendum, "whether you mean it or not," we are both relieved to discover that our anonymous adviser is not such a prig after all and pleased by the sophistication of the newly completed message. In both cases, we could diagram the movement of the joke as follows:

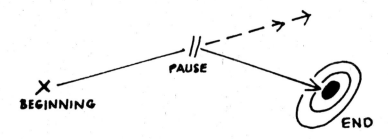

Their line of thought appears to be traveling toward one sort of destination, but it ends up hitting another target altogether.

To put it succinctly, the characteristics that define the procedures of these jokes are the qualities of *surprise* and *fit*; each quip plays a trick on our expectations but puts its topic together in a novel manner.

The combination of these two characteristics—surprise and fit—is common throughout the kingdom of humor. It occurs in many variations, but some form of confounding our preliminary expectations and putting the puzzle together in an unexpected pattern is what humor almost always does.

Show me a poet who leaps up in the morning and gets to work immediately, and I'll show you a man who's going from bed to verse.

Even such a tortured pun as the foregoing operates according to the principles we have outlined. "Going from bed to verse" may amount to nothing more than an insipid play on words, but it does constitute a fitting description of the poet who "leaps up in the morning and gets to work immediately."

Consider what is probably the shortest joke in the English language:

THIMK!

It too comprises both a puzzle and a solution, though here they occur almost simultaneously. For the briefest of instants, we either believe we have seen the word spelled correctly or we don't understand exactly what we are reading. Then the fog lifts and we realize that in the misspelling a satirical point has been made. (To dispel your growing conviction that by now I must have lost what little sense of humor I possessed at the start of this study, I will refrain from spelling it out, but I'm sure you will agree that the explanatory combination, "surprise and fit," fits surprisingly well indeed.)

Now consider the following story:

A young man goes to confession. "Forgive me, Father, for I have sinned," he murmurs. "I have sinned a carnal sin with one of the female members of the congregation."

"Who was it?" asks the priest.

"Oh, I cannot betray that confidence," the young man says.

But the priest is persistent. "Was it, by any chance, the lovely Mrs. Gallagher?"

The young man shakes his head.

"Was it, then, the vivacious Miss Donleavy?"

He shakes his head again.

"Well, was it Murphy's beautiful daughter?"

He still refuses to answer.

On leaving the church, however, he meets a friend outside. "Did Father O'Malley give you absolution?"

"No," says the sinner. "But he did give me three good leads."

The whole story up to the punch line moves in one direction and we do not detect the surprise that is quietly being prepared. When we read the final remark, however, we see that what we had thought made one sort of sense can be interpreted to make another. We have been tricked, but we enjoy it, for whereas one thought-sequence has been snatched away from us, a more ingenious one has been handed us in its place.

This, in essence, is the process or pattern of humor, but simple as it may seem, its implications are highly significant. Whenever we hear a joke, see a ludicrous image, or perceive the ridiculous aspect of a real-life situation, our habitual mental operations are forestalled and new ones are substituted. We are robbed of the opportunity to complete a conventional train of thought and are presented with a more imaginative one in its place. The substitution is amusing, but its ramifications are more than amusing, for they turn us on to the possibility of unique, unstereotyped thinking on a wider scale. Whatever the specific topics of our laughter, in the mere fact of reacting through humor we achieve a moment of nascence, of renewal, of creativity.

This process sheds light on the levitating influence of wit and comedy in general. In *Fiction and the Unconscious*, Simon O. Lesser, comparing comic and tragic literature, says: "Even when comic characters are beset by innumerable troubles, they never give the impression of being trapped, isolated like a tragic hero whose doom is imminent in a small and contracting square of space. The world of comedy adjoins the one we know and is as spacious as that world appears when we are young." Not only is this spaciousness embodied in the characters; it is part of the very structure of humor, which inherently provides the constant possibility of a new, unexpected beginning.

What occurs on the stage or in literature, moreover, is only a dramatization of what may occur in life. And here too the principle holds: seen through the eyes of tragedy, our lives are controlled by immutable forces and there is nothing we can do but live out our fateful destinies; seen through the spectacles of humor, on the other hand, we are capable of shifting gears, reversing direction, seeking new goals, and re-establishing our battered self-respect until the end of our days—and sometimes a little longer.

The procedure of humor, in short, is the procedure of creativity, for, in its construction as well as its content, the ludicrous continually provides us with new compositions formed out of old raw materials. Most ordinary jokes and witticisms strike us as trivia, the pleasant but unimportant overflow of the carefree mind at play. In themselves, many funny remarks may be nothing more than that, but as a body of activity our indulgence in humor facilitates our creative possibilities, for it lubricates the unconventional, imaginative problem-solving functions of our being.

Q: What is purple, dangerous, and lives in a tree?
A: A man-eating plum.

"My doctor is very successful. He specializes in diseases of the rich."

From pure absurdity to pointed barbs, the play of wit puts pieces of thought together to create brand-new ideas. So doing, it pries us loose from encrusted ruts of thinking and invites us to skip along on novel pathways of the mind. It is in this respect that humor paves the way for originality on a wider scale. Silly and childish as it often appears, irreverent and impertinent as it always is, our sense of humor has the power to unlock all our other creative potentials.

Humor, moreover, is not just a key to creativity; it is itself a creative act. Like a scientific theory, a painting, or a poem, even a lowly joke deals in novelty and originality. It rejects conventional thinking, makes use of imagination, and articulates the unheard-of. Conceived, like its more illustrious relatives, in a burst of inspiration, the humorous product too may be shaped and refined in painstaking dedication. While the common currency of laughter seems a far cry from art or science, while it may neither glorify nor explain life the better, it arises out of the same dissatisfaction with the *status quo* and asserts the same right to evolve new forms of thought and imagery.

The kind of humor we would unhesitatingly call creative is produced, more often than not, by recognized comic geniuses. Twain, Thurber, Perelman, Feiffer: these writers, everyone knows, are capable of artistic achievement. It is enlightening, therefore, to discover anonymous works which, while not necessarily brilliant, convincingly display the creative spirit in comic guise. An office memo which was found pinned to the bulletin board of a hospital at which I used to work, ran somewhat as follows:

TO ALL EMPLOYEES OF THIS INSTITUTION:

Due to the undue frequency of absences from work, the following rules are now in effect.

SICKNESS: No excuse. We no longer accept your doctor's statement, as it stands to reason that if you are able to go to the doctor you are able to come to work.

DEATH (OTHER THAN YOUR OWN): No excuse. There is nothing you can do for them, and there is always someone else who can attend to the arrangements.

DEATH (YOUR OWN): This will be accepted as an excuse, provided that you give us two weeks notice, as your contract clearly stipulates.

TOILET: Entirely too much time is being spent in the restrooms. It is imperative, therefore, that you follow the practice of going in alphabetical order. Those whose names begin with "A" can go from 8:00 to 8:30; those whose names begin with "B" can go from 8:30 to 9:00; and so on. Locate your time zone now and regulate yourself accordingly. If you forget to go at your appointed time, it will be necessary, in fairness to your colleagues, to wait until the next day when your turn comes round again.

YOURS FOR BETTER ESPRIT DE CORPS,
THE BOARD OF DIRECTORS.

The disgruntled employees who produced this memorandum may have possessed no exceptional literary talent, but their satirical attack on the prevailing atmosphere in which we worked was nothing short of ingenious to the rest of us.

A humorist who does command literary powers, of course, can amuse a much larger audience with his creations. One of the finest such writers is Ephraim Kishon, a prolific Israeli author, some of whose works have been translated into English. His short story "Jewish Poker" is without doubt a comic gem.

Jewish Poker

For quite a while the two of us sat at our table, wordlessly stirring our coffee. Ervinke was bored.

"All right," he said. "Let's play poker."

"No," I answered. "I hate cards. I always lose."

"Who's talking about cards?" thus Ervinke. "I was thinking of Jewish poker."

He then briefly explained the rules of the game. Jewish poker is played without cards, in your head, as befits the People of the Book.

"You think of a number, I also think of a number," Ervinke said. "Whoever thinks of a higher number wins. This sounds easy, but it has a hundred pitfalls. Nu!"

"All right," I agreed. "Let's try."

We plunked down five piasters each, and leaning back in our chairs began to think of numbers. After a while Ervinke signaled that he had one. I said I was ready.

"All right," thus Ervinke. "Let's hear your number."

"Eleven," I said.

"Twelve," Ervinke said, and took the money. I could have kicked myself, because originally I had thought of Fourteen, and only at the last moment had I climbed down to Eleven, I really don't know why.

"Listen." I turned to Ervinke. "What would have happened had I said Fourteen?"

"What a question! I'd have lost. Now, that is just the charm of poker: you never know how things will turn out. But if your nerves cannot stand a little gambling, perhaps we had better call it off."

Without saying another word, I put down ten piasters on the table. Ervinke did likewise. I pondered my number carefully and opened with Eighteen.

"Damn!" Ervinke said. "I have only Seventeen!"

I swept the money into my pocket and quietly guffawed. Ervinke had certainly not dreamed that I would master the tricks of Jewish poker so quickly. He had probably counted on my opening with Fifteen or Sixteen, but certainly not with Eighteen. Ervinke, his brow in angry furrows, proposed we double the stakes.

"As you like," I sneered, and could hardly keep back my jubilant laughter. In the meantime a fantastic number had occurred to me: Thirty-five!

"Lead!" said Ervinke.

"Thirty-five!"

"Forty-three!"

With that he pocketed the forty piasters. I could feel the blood rushing into my brain.

"Listen," I hissed. "Then why didn't you say Forty-three the last time?"

"Because I had thought of Seventeen!" Ervinke retorted indignantly. "Don't you see, that is the fun in poker: you never know what will happen next."

"A pound," I remarked dryly, and, my lips curled in scorn, I threw a note on the table. Ervinke extracted a similar note from his pocket and with maddening slowness placed it next to mine. The tension was unbearable. I opened with Fifty-four.

"Oh, damn it!" Ervinke fumed. "I also thought of Fifty-four! Draw! Another game!"

My brain worked with lightning speed. "Now you think I'll again call Eleven, my boy," I reasoned. "But you'll get the surprise of your life." I chose the sure-fire Sixty-nine.

"You know what, Ervinke"—I turned to Ervinke—"you lead."

"As you like," he agreed. "It's all the same with me. Seventy!"

Everything went black before my eyes. I had not felt such panic since the seige of Jerusalem.

"Nu?" Ervinke urged. "What number did you think of?"

"What do you know?" I whispered with downcast eyes. "I have forgotten."

"You liar!" Ervinke flared up. "I know you didn't forget, but simply thought of a smaller number and now don't want to own up. An old trick. Shame on you!"

I almost slapped his loathsome face for this evil slander, but with some difficulty overcame the urge. With blazing eyes I upped the stakes by another pound and thought of a murderous number: Ninety-six!

"Lead, stinker," I threw at Ervinke, *whereupon he leaned across the table and hissed into my face:*

"Sixteen hundred and eighty-three!"

A queer weakness gripped me.

"Eighteen hundred," I mumbled wearily.

"Double!" Ervinke shouted, and pocketed the four pounds.

"What do you mean, 'double'?" I snorted. "What's that?"

"If you lose your temper in poker, you'll lose your shirt!" Ervinke lectured me. "Any child will understand that my number doubled is higher than yours, so it's clear that . . ."

"Enough," I gasped, and threw down a fiver. *"Two thousand,"* I led.

"Two thousand four hundred and seventeen," thus Ervinke.

"Double!" I sneered, and grabbed the stakes, but Ervinke caught my hand.

"Redouble!" he whispered, and pocketed the tenner. *I felt I was going out of my mind.*

"Listen"—I gritted my teeth—"if that's how things stand, I could also have said 'redouble' in the last game, couldn't I?"

"Of course," Ervinke agreed. "To tell you the truth, I was rather surprised that you didn't. But this is poker, yahabibi, *you either know how to play it or you don't! If you are scatterbrained, better stick to croquet."*

The stakes were ten pounds. "Lead!" I screamed. Ervinke leaned back in his chair, and in a disquietingly calm voice announced his number: Four.

"Ten million!" I blared triumphantly. But without the slightest sign of excitement, Ervinke said:

"Ultimo!"

And took the twenty pounds.

I then broke into sobs. Ervinke stroked my hair and told me that according to Hoyle, whoever is first out with the ultimo wins, regardless of numbers. That is the fun in poker: you have to make split-second decisions.

"Twenty pounds," I whimpered, and placed my last notes in the hands of fate. *Ervinke also placed his money. My face was bathed in cold sweat. Ervinke went on calmly blowing smoke rings, only his eyes had narrowed.*

"Who leads?"

"You," I answered, and he fell into my trap like the sucker he was.

"So I lead," Ervinke said. "Ultimo," and he stretched out his hand for the treasure.

"Just a moment"—I stopped him—"Ben-Gurion!"

With that I pocketed the Mint's six-month output. "Ben-Gurion is even stronger than ultimo," I explained. "But it's getting dark outside. Perhaps we had better break it off."

We paid the waiter and left.

Ervinke asked for his money back, saying that I had invented the Ben-Gurion on the spur of the moment. I admitted this, but said that the fun in poker was just in the rule that you never returned the money you had won.

An inspired flight of fancy such as this deserves, in every sense of the term, to be called a creative achievement. And even though lesser efforts may fail to match its excellence, we must perceive the selfsame impulse involved in their production. The exercise of wit, professional or amateur, is an exercise in originality. From the most sublime expressions of the comic spirit down to its most vulgar forms, it provides a vehicle for the inventive urge, for humor is, in its fundamental process, an inherently creative enterprise.

Telling
Jokes

The telling of jokes appears to be a trivial form of communication. Though we all like to hear a few "good ones" and envy the individual who tells them well, we rarely believe that anything of consequence occurs in the event. The activity, however, is common to all cultures, so it may, despite appearances, fulfill a significant function in the human community-at-large. If we examine the motives which inspire us to tell each other jokes and the techniques we employ in doing so, we will attain a vantage point from which we can better estimate the importance of this transaction.

To begin at the beginning, let us note that the earliest, most elementary laughter-producing stimulus is not a joke at all; it is a tickle. Some wit has asserted that the tickle is about as relevant to humor as the onion is to tragedy, but we need not accept his argument with more than a chuckle of assent. Tickling awakens laughter in people of all ages, so it may very well shed light on the phenomenon of joking.

How and why, then, do we tickle each other? The how we all know: a light, periodic jabbing or stroking of sensitive areas of the body. The why is more debatable. When we tickle an infant or a little child, our pleasure may simply reside in the communication of an exciting, enlivening experience. The child giggles, the tickler laughs, and both share a jolly time. When one child tickles another, though, the character of the interchange may become more aggressive. Since tickling easily shades off into discomfort, it frequently develops into a cloaked attack in which, under the guise of innocent merriment, one person takes delight in inflicting pain on another. When adults engage in tickling, moreover, the motive pattern may take on a distinctly sexual tone. Lovers excite each other, or a wooer attempts to arouse the object of his desire, by the use of this primitive device.

Interestingly enough, both the techniques and motives involved in tickling have their counterparts in the telling of jokes. With regard to technique: jokes aimed at sensitive parts of our minds, at topics about which we feel some anxiety, are always more effective than jokes aimed at undefended territory. And the jabbing or stroking approach, with the swift alternation of tension and release that it engenders, is analogous to the effect of visual or verbal humor. Here, too, the jokester provokes a state of tension as he builds up his story and a moment of release when he delivers the punch line. The motivational analogies are even more apparent; wit is frequently employed as a cloaked attack, a means of sexual arousal, and a form of shared exuberance.

Another kind of laughter-producing activity also precedes true humor. Trickery or practical joking is practiced by youngsters, and sometimes adults, the world over. It may take the form of a physical act—putting a tack on the teacher's chair or surreptitiously tripping a friend—or it may be a verbal maneuver. One child asks another, "What's the difference between a mailbox and a garbage can?" When the one who has been asked admits he doesn't know, the trickster replies, "Then I'll never send you to mail a letter." The interchange may take on lewd overtones as well. When I was in high school, one of my pals won the admiration of the other boys by "putting on" our female teachers with such vulgar gambits as the following:

Student (sotto voce): "Miss ——, may I please tickle your ass with a broom?"

Teacher (perplexed): "I beg your pardon?"

Student (all innocence): "May I please ask to leave the room?"

Like tickling, trickery presages more sophisticated forms of wit. As is the case with so many jokes, it both surprises the recipient and provides an aggressive and/or sexual release for the perpetrator. The difference between playing practical jokes and telling funny stories, in fact, boils down to little more than a shift from using the recipient as a victim to inviting him to become an audience. This slight shift, however, is of the utmost importance, for it signifies nothing less than a change from barbarous to civilized behavior. On the level of trickery, the relationship between the perpetrator and the recipient is totally competitive, while on the level of comedy it becomes cooperative. Rather than attack his listeners, the joke-teller invites them to join him in verbally, not physically, attacking others or, on a yet more refined level, to share amusing thoughts attacking no one at all.

These preliminary considerations have now put us in an advantageous position from which to analyze the techniques and motives involved in telling jokes. Like children's behavior in general, both tickling and trickery reveal the crude feelings that lie behind our comic adult communications. They show that the most sublime humor arises out of the earth of undifferentiated excitement, aggression, and sexuality. Since the analogies between tickling, trickery, and comedy are clear, we may anticipate that the telling of jokes will have much in common with the sharing of exuberance and the release of aggression and sex.

Proper timing, it is often said, is one of the technical factors the joke-teller has to master. What exactly is proper timing, and why is it so important? The pace or tempo of relating a story or delivering a quip and, in particular, the pause between the buildup and the twist are what the matter amounts to. Tempos may vary from leisurely to rapid, but the effective jokester always operates within an awareness of building up expectations in his audience and then suddenly surprising them. Functioning within this framework, he must increase their tension to a point of suspense and then provide the release. He goes wrong if he either fails to generate sufficient suspense or delays too long in providing relief.

Since a joke is, as we have shown, the transposition of a trick, the listener must be caught unaware for the trick to come off. This is one reason why jokes—in constrast to, say, poems—are enjoyed so much less the second time around, and it is one reason why written humor is less effective than the spoken or acted variety.

The importance of proper timing is clearly easier to illustrate in person than in writing, but we can give it a try nonetheless:

A man is telling his friend why he has never married. "Every girl I bring home," he says, "my mother doesn't like. They're either too tall or too short, too fat or too thin, too smart or too dumb, too loud or too quiet. I just can't seem to please her."

"Well," his friend replies, "I'll tell you what to do. Keep looking till you find a girl who closely resembles your mother herself. Then she can't find fault with her."

The man agrees, and a month later he meets his friend again. "I followed your advice," he says. "I looked and looked until I found a girl who was just like my mother. The same height, the same weight, the same personality, the same mind."

"Yes yes, and what happened?"

"My father couldn't stand her."

By interfering with its timing, the identical story can be rendered much less potent. For example.

A man is telling his friend why he has never married. "Every girl I bring home," he says, "my mother doesn't care for. No matter what they're like, she always finds something to criticize."

"Well," says the friend, "keep looking till you find a girl who resembles your mother herself. Then she can't find fault with her."

The man agrees, and a month later he meets his friend again. "I followed your advice," he says. "I found a girl who was just like my mother. Unfortunately, however, I asked my father what he thought of her, and he said he couldn't stand her."

The same point is made, but the second version falls flatter than the first because its element of surprise is less accentuated. Both the buildup of descriptive traits and the sudden introduction of the punch line in the first version heighten its effectiveness; the relative lack of buildup and the gradual introduction of the punch line in the second make it far the weaker joke.

Next to timing, caricature is crucial to the joke-teller's craft. The exaggerated verisimilitude with which he renders his characters' characters can spell the difference between a guffaw and a yawn. The gifted mimic is therefore well-endowed to play the part of the comic and anyone who can imitate the mannerisms of others is on his way to telling jokes successfully.

Many stand-up comedians bank heavily on their skill in the art of caricature. As a result, the effectiveness of their stories depends as much on their portrayals as on the specific events they relate. When Bill Cosby describes his boyhood encounters with Fat Albert, the neighborhood slob, we laugh as heartily at the image of this lumbering ox as at the witticisms Cosby tosses our way. When any one of a host of comics stiffens his spine, purses his lips, and launches a take-off on Ed Sullivan, we chuckle as soon as we see the familiar gait and grimaces reproduced before our eyes.

In creating a parodied likeness of his target, the joke-teller sets the stage for his joke, since caricature in itself spotlights the oddness of its butts. By reflecting, in magnified proportions, a person's prominent features, it distorts his normality and emphasizes his ridiculousness. His awkwardness, his ugliness, his stupidity, or his pomposity: these are the traits that are graphically portrayed. We laugh at them because they allow us to feel superior to the unfortunate, pilloried victim.

Elegance, finally, rounds out the basic repertoire of the jokester's formal techniques. The neatness with which he delivers his sallies distinguishes his ability as much as any other trait. If he stumbles, loses track, or hems and haws, he might as well give up the calling. If, however, his wit flows smoothly from his lips, if his thought skips nimbly to its appointed destination, he is on the road to comic acclaim.

In writing, too, the elegance of a joke's construction enhances its effectiveness:

I wish I were now what I was when I wanted to be what I am now.

Help, Help! The paranoids are after me!

Guard against Frrors!

It would be difficult to render any one of these witticisms in a neater fashion, and it is for this very reason that they strike us as tiny gems.

To this point, we have been focusing on what we might call the compositional aspects of the joke-teller's art. Equally important, however, are the content categories his wit taps, for the effectiveness of a joke depends in large part on the strength of the drives it releases in the listener.

Aggression and sex are the most common beneficiaries of humor. The joker who knows how to prime these two pumps is assured of a responsive audience, unless his approach is too gross for their sensibilities.

A man and wife are watching television. There is a knock at the door. The man calls out, "Who's there?" A voice answers, "It's the Boston Strangler." Turning to his wife, the man says, "It's for you, dear."

Arriving home unexpectedly, a husband finds his wife in bed with another man. "See here," he shouts. "Just what do you think you're doing?" "You see?" says the wife to the man beside her. "Didn't I tell you he was stupid?"

Both these stories may be tasteless, but we find them funny because they touch us where we live. They evoke a gut reaction, though they may not rate too high in intelligence or wit. Humor liberates many other kinds of drives, as the first part of this book should have made clear, but when it triggers our lust and hostility its potency is strongest.

In general, we may also note, any joke or witty remark that helps reduce anxiety is bound to be found enjoyable. More than one professional comic has taken advantage of the public's fear of flying by creating comic routines that purge this particular fear. Whoever originated the monologue, "Don't worry. Flying is not dangerous. Crashing is dangerous, but flying is not dangerous," knew exactly how to get to us. On the ground or in a plane, many people experience trepidation about air travel; as a result, we are prone to appreciate remarks that make fun of its risks. Were we aboard an aircraft in serious trouble, of course, it is unlikely that we could tolerate witty observations on the event, but as long as the prospect is theoretical we enjoy making light of it. Some measure of anxiety promotes our responsiveness to humor, though too great a degree obliterates it entirely.

Appropriateness, we all know, is highly important too. An election joke told around election time is far more effective than the same joke told at another time. An educational anecdote at which a television audience would not even chuckle might be found uproarious by a convention of teachers.

A spontaneous witticism, therefore, that is tailor-made to suit the occasion is always funnier than a story that has been constructed beforehand. "How do you feel?" said a real-life nurse to a blood donor as she was drawing the sample from his arm. "I feel like I want to go home," he replied. While hardly ingenious, the unrehearsed declaration struck both of them as hilarious.

Contrived jokes, too, are increased in effectiveness when they are linked to current concerns. Many old Jewish stories, for this very reason, are now being widely retold with a cast of Negro characters. They fit any underprivileged minority group but, since today the black man wears that mantle more than the Jew, it is obviously more appropriate to have the stories depict his predicament.

Two Negroes meet in the street. "Howzit goin', baby?" asks the first.
"R-r-r-rough, man!" says the second. "I j-j-j-just lost out on a job 'cause of bein' black."
"Sonofabitch," says the first. "Ain't it always the way. What was the job, baby? Somethin' cool?"
"Y-y-you said it, man. J-j-just what I always ·wanted. R-r-r-radio announcer."

(Original version: Two Jews meet in the street. "How have you been, Moishe?" asks the first.
"N-n-not bad," says the second. "B-but I had an unfortunate experience. I l-l-l-lost a job I was hoping to get as a r-r-r-radio announcer."
"That's a shame," agrees the first. "But what can you expect?"
And they both throw up their hands and say in unison, "Antisemitism!")

In combination with all these factors, it is significant that the two extremes, utter candor and absurdity, are both surefire material for humor. Let a man enunciate the feelings and thoughts we are too polite or squeamish to admit, and he will evoke a laugh by this gesture alone. Let him, in contrast, bring ludicrous, nonsensical images into our minds and he will evoke the same response.

Two people are engaged in earnest conversation. One is explaining in detail his theories about the current fiscal crisis. The other nods in agreement and murmurs, from time to time, "You're right ... Yes, of course ... I feel that way too." After a little while, the one who is doing all the talking pauses and says, "Well now, what exactly would you suggest?" Sheepishly, the other confesses, "To tell the truth, I wasn't listening."

Imagine, in comparison, a totally different kind of event.

A father is blowing up balloons for his children. He inflates each balloon into a beautiful round bubble and sends it floating round the room. When he reaches the final one, however, he is almost out of wind. With a mighty effort, he blows it up but, before he can tie its end, it deflates back into him and he goes floating round the room.

Both situations, we must agree, are mildly humorous. Yet on the surface they seem like opposites. In the first, we are treated to candor, in the second to absurdity. What they have in common, however, and what makes them equally funny, is the fact that they depart from reality as we know it—not from real, honest-to-goodness truth but from the way people usually behave. And that, in sum, is probably the basic criterion for humorous material: do or say something different, something unexpected and a little shocking, and in that moment you become a comic character.

So much for the techniques of telling jokes. Now what are the motives that impel us to do it? Why do we like to make each other laugh?

When children and adolescents are asked to name the qualities they admire in their friends, they almost always put "a good sense of humor" near the top of the list. As adults, too, we enjoy the company of people who amuse us. Seeing the widespread appeal of humor, then, it seems obvious that we would want to practice it. Since we all desire popularity, we may feel inclined to tell jokes or come up with funny remarks on that basis alone. Then, the more response we receive, the more are we reinforced in doing it, until it becomes a habitual way of gaining recognition and applause.

But there is a set of deeper, less obvious motives involved as well. A great deal of humor, as we have seen, is distinctly hostile in content, and we cannot deny that the pleasure we derive from relating these kinds of stories or making these kinds of remarks partakes of the feelings being communicated. To express hostile thoughts and get away with it, to display aggressive impulses and have them accepted by a delighted audience, is clearly a boon to be cherished.

Perhaps an equal number of jokes are sexually provocative, and here too our pleasure partakes of the feelings being aired. We achieve the titillation of mental exhibitionism, we revel in the arousal of our listeners' concupiscence, and once again we garner the boon of having our unacceptable fantasies accepted.

Humor's role as an agent of sublimation must not be underestimated. It welds the human community together, for it allows us to confess our secret vices and to assure each other, in our responsive laughter, that we are all in the very same boat. When one individual tells any joke, or makes any witty remark that reveals raw, uncivilized feelings, and another individual reacts with mirth, a bond is created between them—a bond that affirms that they understand and accept each other's being on a level more basic than words.

That, in short, is probably the basic motive underlying the telling of jokes, and it brings us back, curiously enough, to the earliest motive underlying the practice of tickling: a sharing of exuberance, of excitement, of joy. The fun two human beings in sensitive communion can generate between themselves is what it all comes down to. We make ourselves happy by making each other happy. And why not? We are all so capable of making each other miserable that the telling of jokes, or the communication of humor in general, seems an indispensable balance in the seesaw of human relations.

Discovering
Ourselves
Through Laughter

There are many keyholes into the psyche. Dreams, slips of the tongue, neurotic symptoms, likes and dislikes: each has been used as a peephole through which to observe the activity in the "little black box" of our being. By studying these often peculiar manifestations, psychologists have managed to illuminate the darker corners of our minds.

Our sense of humor is one such keyhole, but it has never yet been systematically employed to shed light on our inner selves. For all the theorizing and research that has been done on humor, we are not yet in a position to formulate, with any certainty, a method of using it as a self-exploratory device.

In this chapter, I intend to put forth some preliminary suggestions along this line. I will describe a number of ways in which our sense of humor can be used, as our dreams have been used, to clarify certain aspects of our personalities. Whether other psychologists will find these suggestions stimulating to their own work remains to be seen; whether the layman can use them to analyze himself is equally open to question. My only purpose here is to start the ball rolling in a direction which one day may prove worth the while.

Let us begin with the proposition that what we laugh at has both collective and personal significance. Certain images and events are found funny by almost everyone in our society. Certain classes of events, indeed, are found funny by all peoples in all cultures whatsoever. A supposedly respectable person doing or saying something shocking but not seriously harmful; a conceited or pompous person having his dignity besmirched; an absurd remark or action: these things seem to be perceived as humorous in every country on the map. Within this framework, however, more specific kinds of events are found more amusing by Orientals than Occidentals, by Englishmen than Germans, by radical Americans than reactionary Americans. And narrowing it down to the nub, certain definite expressions and actions are reacted to with greater hilarity by one individual than another.

The standard, collective phenomena that everyone finds funny reveal our collective dynamics. Since we all laugh at a pompous person having his dignity besmirched, we may infer that we all resent pomposity in others, find it oppressive and irritating, and therefore appreciate its downfall. Since we also laugh at unconventional behavior, we may infer that we labor under the restrictions of conventionality and enjoy its occasional overthrow.

Among these collective phenomena, however, each of us seems to have certain preferences. Some of us clearly enjoy hostile wit more than others; some dwell persistently on off-color stories; some love absurdity or philosophical humor. Our preferences, we may assume, reflect the state of our psychic economy. The person whose wit is consistently sarcastic is, in all probability, engaged in working off an accumulation of resentful feelings. Apparently he harbors a cargo of anger which he is attempting to unload. The individual, in contrast, who eschews this kind of expression may either be experiencing little resentment or be so desperately afraid of displaying it that even the roundabout avenue of wit is too frightening for him to follow. The same line of reasoning may be applied to people who either prefer or avoid sexual humor: those who continually indulge in it probably need a continual release of their promiscuous impulses, while those who recoil from it probably cannot accept the fact that they have these impulses. The person, finally, who appreciates absurdity or philosophical wit more than any other kind is, in all likelihood, deeply involved with his thinking processes and touchy about having any of his vital emotions exposed. It seems significant, in this regard, that both young children and intellectuals appear to have a strong attraction to nonsense humor. On the one hand, the children are just beginning to experience the workings of their reasoning powers; on the other hand, the intellectuals are satiated with them. Both groups, therefore, are inclined to toy with reason and get a special thrill out of its abrogation.

As an informal test of our own preferences, let us attempt to rate our reactions to the following jokes. Having done so, we will discuss the implications of our responses.

Simply check the area in the scale that seems closest to your feelings about the joke.

1. Love is a disease that creates its own antibody: marriage.

very funny ⌞|⌞|⌞|⌞|⌞⌟ not funny

2. Q: What does a 500-lb. canary say?
A: CHURP!

very funny ⌞|⌞|⌞|⌞|⌞⌟ not funny

3. A famous actor is accosted by a whore. He spends the night at her place. When he is leaving, she says, "But you didn't give me anything." So he gives her two tickets to a matinee. She objects, "I don't want to see a show. I'm hungry. I need bread." To which he replies, "If you need bread, screw the baker. From me you get tickets to the theater."

very funny ⌞|⌞|⌞|⌞|⌞⌟ not funny

4. "Mama, Mama—daddy's on fire!"
"Okay, honey—get the marshmallows."

very funny ⌞|⌞|⌞|⌞|⌞⌟ not funny

5. Q: What's red and white and goes, "putt-putt-putt"?
A: An outboard radish.

very funny ⌞|⌞|⌞|⌞|⌞⌟ not funny

6. When two politicians accuse each other of lying, both of them are telling the truth.

very [| | | | |] not
funny   funny

7. Sign on a brothel door:
OUT TO LUNCH
GO F—K YOURSELF

very [| | | | |] not
funny   funny

8. A philosopher, in the throes of death, moans, "What's the answer? What's the answer?"

His colleague, who is attending to his needs, shrugs his shoulders and replies, "What's the question?"

very [| | | | |] not
funny   funny

9. Patient: Please help me, doctor. I'm afraid I'm losing my memory.

Doctor: Mmm—mmm. And how long have you had this problem?

Patient: What problem?

very [| | | | |] not
funny   funny

10. A farmer is showing a beautiful lady visitor around his farm. They watch a bull lustily mating a cow. Putting

his arm around the lady's waist, the farmer says, "Boy, I'd sure like to do something like that." "Well, why don't you?" she replies. "It's your cow."

very funny |__|__|__|__|__| not funny

11. Advice to the overweight: Want to lose ten pounds of ugly, useless fat? Cut off your head.

very funny |__|__|__|__|__| not funny

12. A group of scientists developed the ultimate computer. They decide, therefore, to ask it the ultimate question: "Is there a god?" The computer whirrs and clicks, its lights blink, and finally its message appears. It reads: "Now there is."

very funny |__|__|__|__|__| not funny

If you have attempted to rate your reactions to these jokes, you have probably experienced some confusion. Some of the jokes may have seemed clever but not laughable, others may have moved you to laughter and yet you may have thought them stupid or gross. Besides that, if you had heard one before, it may have been difficult to compare it to one you were hearing for the first time. Rating problems such as these beset all research on humor. Since our present aim is not to devise an impeccable scientific study, however, we can ignore them for the time being. We need only note that we do indeed have preferences in humor, and we need only pursue the notion that if we can locate them we may discover something interesting about ourselves.

In the series of jokes above, numbers 1, 8, and 12 may be called philosophical; numbers 2, 5, and 9 may be called nonsensical; numbers 3, 7, and 10 may be called sexual; and numbers 4, 6, and 11 may be called hostile. Those of us who show a clearcut preference or a clearcut distaste for any one of these categories should consider what that means with regard to our personality dynamics. As we have already mentioned, a special affinity to certain types of humor indicates an unusual need to work off anxiety related to its content, while a strong dislike suggests an inability to tolerate irreverance about its content.

Those of us who did not rate any one of the categories listed above as most or least appealing should now do a little introspection to see if we can define our humorous preferences in everyday life. Many of us are inclined to claim that we react to every joke we hear on its merits alone—that we do not love or hate it because it has relevance to our personal needs—but that claim is frequently specious. We all know that Democrats admire witticisms that put down Republicans, that pupils love remarks that ridicule teachers, that Jews enjoy Jewish jokes and Catholics Catholic jokes, that married men guffaw at stories satirizing marriage, that doctor jokes appeal to all of us because we all have some anxiety about the prospect of medical treatment. What we are suggesting here is simply that our preferences may spread out on a wider scale as well. Not only may we have a special need to laugh at doctors, teachers, wives, and politicians, but emotional states such as a buildup of hostility or guilt over sex may also be involved in our humorous reactions.

Much more significant than our humorous reactions, however, are our humorous creations. The spontaneous witticisms we come up with ourselves grow directly out of our personal predicaments. They represent one of our natural ways of coping with anxiety and they reveal, as clear as day, the internal pressures out of which they have been conceived.

At the end of a hard-fought tennis match, the loser kids the winner, "Don't worry, pal. You'll do better next time." What has motivated the remark? In all probability, he feels disappointed at having lost and is attempting to restore his self-esteem. By jokingly adopting the patronizing attitude of a victor, he soothes the pain of defeat and transcends his humiliation. Psychologists may call it an ego-defensive maneuver and, scrutinized soberly, it may seem pathetic, but it is an effective coping mechanism. Rather than curse or cry or make excuses, rather than take life's blows without a murmur, we all have the capability of healing our wounds with humor. Many of our spur-of-the-moment funny remarks have this function. They represent defensive reactions to wounded vanity or to the threat of wounded vanity.

If we agree that spontaneous humor is revealing, each of us might attempt to assess his own brand of humor to see where it leads. More than likely, however, we would find the assessment difficult to carry out. As elusive as the task of recording our dreams and fantasies, recalling and analyzing our humorous creations is like pursuing a will-o'-the wisp. Still, for those who may wish to try, here are a few suggestions.

Spontaneous humor may dwell on specific topics, such as the joker's wife or boss or his intelligence or sexual prowess.

If it does, rest assured that the topic is in some important sense a source of anxiety.

Spontaneous humor may occupy broader categories, such as the four we applied to our list of jokes: philosophical, nonsensical, sexual, and hostile. If it concentrates on any one or more of these, draw your own conclusions on the basis of what we said about them earlier.

Spontaneous humor may also be assessed in terms of its emphasis on laughter at others, laughter at impersonal events, or laughter at oneself. Laughter directed at others usually displays hostility or envy; it shows a need to raise our self-esteem by ridiculing our competitors. Laughter at impersonal events—plays-on-words, odd coincidences, ludicrous images— is much like "art for art's sake"; it expresses an enjoyment of humor for itself, for the pure amusement of lightheartedness and lightheadedness. Laughter at oneself reveals self-doubt or guilt; it represents an attempt to rise above both inferiority and superiority feelings and to accept ourselves for what we are.

Of course, our spontaneous humor may fluctuate. One week or one year we may find ourselves taking many witty jabs at our friends and neighbors, while at another time we may come out with neutral or self-directed observations. What the flow of our wit reflects are the ups and downs of our psychic economy. The precise nature of the relationship, as we pointed out at the beginning of this chapter, is still only dimly understood. Yet we may proceed on the assurance that some relationship does in fact exist, and at times, we may also note, the correspondence of an individual's sense of humor to other aspects of his being is dramatically apparent.

The most vivid example I can recall occurred at a raucous New Year's Eve party many years ao. Most of the guests were more than mildly inebriated and, as the conversation grew less and less inhibited, someone told a joke dealing with oral intercourse. All present reacted with moderate laughter—all, that is, except one couple. The husband of this pair practically slid off his seat in hilarity; he shrieked and guffawed, clutched his sides, and rolled about in delight. The wife, at the same time, became so flustered that she had to leave the room. I learned at a later date what you may have already deduced. This couple, newly married, had been guiltily experimenting with this form of sexual activity and both felt extremely anxious about it. When the joke was told, it provided a powerful catharsis for the husband but came too close for comfort for the wife.

Through events like this may be rare, if we take a careful look at our own response to humor and, especially, at our original humorous observations, there is no doubt that we will glimpse, as through a revealing aperture, the secret workings of our inner selves.

Humor
and
Fanaticism

In many ways, our sense of humor and our propensity for fervent commitment to a cause or belief lie at opposite poles of our being. Commitment presupposes some degree of blind faith; to humor nothing is sacred. Commitment is fueled by passion; humor runs on detachment. Commitment leads to action; humor encourages reflection. Commitment cultivates pride; humor sows humility. The two, it would seem, contradict each other up and down the line. The activation of either one, therefore, should presumably obliterate the other.

Their relationship, however, is more complex and variable than it appears at first glance. Like love and hate, they sometimes coexist or even reinforce each other in unusual ways. As a lover may, in some respect, despise the woman he adores, a "true believer" may perceive, in some dim recess of his mind, the ridiculousness of his flaming devotion to his cause.

The fanatic, it is generally believed, lacks a sense of humor, especially with regard to the subject of his fanaticism. The religious zealot, the righteous patriot, the racial bigot, and the black power militant are all, it is said, incapable of laughing at the particular topic about which they feel so intensely. This assertion stands to reason, for laughter would soften their single-mindedness and waylay their unswerving drive. In actuality, too, the pattern is frequently observed: the dedicated individual sees nothing funny in his dedication. To him, it is as serious as life and death, and he can no more laugh at it than the rest of us can laugh at our demise.

In elaboration of this point of view, the fanatic, it is claimed, employs his wit, if at all, to lacerate his opposition. Caucasian bigots tell vicious jokes comparing Negroes to subhuman creatures, while black militants regale themselves with stories ridiculing lily-livered Whitey. Jewish lore is stocked with anecdotes mocking Christians, and many an Irishman has entertained his friends with anti-Semitic gibes. Such behavior has always been widespread and it seems to clinch the argument that, where chauvinism rules, true humor—in contradistinction to hostile wit—is unable to take root.

Despite its self-evident cogency, however, the argument is not indisputable. In fact, the most fervent crusader is capable, if only with great reluctance, of perceiving the irony of his crusade, and the most narrow-minded chauvinist is able, when sufficiently disarmed, to laugh at his own strutting arrogance. In public, we may all be unwilling to acknowledge any levity about our passionate concerns; in the company of trusted friends, however, we sometimes dare to satirize our most deeply held convictions.

A traditional Jewish story, enjoyed and retold by generations of the orthodox, goes as follows:

A very religious Jew, visiting a relative in another town, tells him:
"Our rabbi is so holy that he talks with God."
"Talks with God!? How do you know that?"
"How do we know? Why, he told us so himself."
"But perhaps he lied."
"Idiot! Would a man who talks with God tell lies?"

An equally pertinent tale, preserved and enjoyed by the very people it satirizes, has a Jew discoursing with the proprietor of a shop selling Jewish religious articles:

"I'd like to see a tallus *(i.e. a prayer shawl), please."*
"All right. What kind are you interested in?"
"Something beautiful and genuine. Made in Israel, if possible. Real silk, too, like the highest rabbis wear."
"I have just the thing. Here, how do you like it?"
"Fine. I'll take it. But wrap it up nice. It's a Christmas present."

This achievement—the capacity for laughter at the very source and substance of our pride—requires an unusually broad-minded outlook, an ability to be passionately involved and lightheartedly detached at the same time. Such a frame of mind may seem, in a sense, schizophrenic, yet it is anything but pathological. All of us, in fact, experience it more frequently than we are willing to admit. Engaged in ardent love-making, for instance, we sometimes play host to extraneous thoughts. At a funeral, too, while crying with grief, we wonder how long the service will last. And in a heated argument, shouting and cursing furiously, we may become aware of the impressive spectacle of our rage. We hate to confess these anomalies because they undermine our pride, but just as we are capable of producing them, so are we capable of feeling intensely and blithely in intimate juxtaposition. We may deny it vociferously or refuse to comprehend it but, just as our laughter is often a cloak for our sadness, beneath our passion our sense of humor lies in wait.

These observations are clearly of more than academic interest. They may be utilized in situations of social crisis where inflamed emotions threaten to result in destructive encounters, for they suggest that, if the participants' sense of humor can be aroused, their zealousness may be modified and tragic happenings avoided. At least one such instance has already been reported in the press. The *New York Times* (November 6, 1967) described an incident in West Berlin in which the police successfully dispersed a student demonstration by adopting a quasi-humorous approach. While preparing to turn water cannons on the demonstrators, the policeman in charge of the operation announced, "Please move on or be prepared to get your bathrobes and towels ready. We are now going to have to stage some unusual aquatics." His handling of the rest of his assignment was conducted in an equally jovial fashion, and the crowd eventually left without either side having inflicted damage or injury on the other.

In this particular instance, two factors coincided to produce the peaceful dispersal. First, the students' commitment to their cause, while sincere and heartfelt, had not reached riotous proportions and, second, the kind of wit the policeman practiced was jocular and easygoing. Both factors are probably important in the use of humor as a technique for quenching hot-headed fanaticism. When feelings are merely simmering, laughter can help to dissipate them, but once they boil over into explosive action it is unlikely to prove successful. At the same time, sarcastic wit directed at the fanatic is hardly like to mollify him, but lighthearted bantering or self-directed humor expressed by either side may very well be effective in cooling antagonisms.

Consider the possibility of a police captain in America addressing a mass of peace marchers over his megaphone:

> *"Ladies and gentlemen, this is the captain of your local pigs. I just want to welcome you to our twenty-fifth confrontation and tell you that, despite my fellow officers' innate lack of sensitivity—not to speak of intelligence—we intend to do our best to see that you enjoy yourselves and accomplish your objectives, as long as those objectives don't amount to wrecking anybody's property or inciting anyone to riot. . . ."*

Or consider the impression a radical student leader might make if he were to communicate with repressive police in these terms.

> *"Speaking on behalf of all the long-haired freaks, I want to thank you for taking the time to supervise our annual picnic and invite you to join in the general merriment after all the boring speeches are over. . . ."*

A willingness to relate in this fahion, of course, presupposes some degree of emotional detachment. It presupposes an ability to adopt a playful attitude in the midst of a grim situation. Anyone who takes himself too seriously would not even contemplate it. The point to note, however, is that humor, like love or anger, tends to be highly contagious. If, as we argued earlier, it exists as an imminent potential beneath the most un-humorous of attitudes, it can probably be pricked into being by sufficient indication that it would be welcomed and, once expressed, it is apt to spread rapidly throughout the vicinity.

When we laugh together, moreover, we all feel closer to one another. Like affectionate physical contact, laughing at the same things brings us more in touch with each other than intellectual agreement. Our sense of humor roots deeper than our reasoning ability, so sharing it gives us a feeling communion at the level of our basic needs.

Both fanaticism and humor spring from a common source. Both represent reactions to frustration, instinctive ways of attempting to cope with distress. When we feel downtrodden and deprived, when our self-esteem is wounded and our needs are unfulfilled, we are prone to latch on to a cause or belief that promises to change the world. In throwing ourselves into "the good fight," we find a new reason for living, give direction to our energies, and revive the hope that reality will be more to our liking in the future. Strangely enough, in similar circumstances we can also take the opposite tack. Rather than try to change the world, we may begin to mock it. By laughing at the selfishness and injustice that prevails, we make ourselves less vulnerable to the torments of defeat. When we don't give a damn about what we haven't got, not having it becomes a minor inconvenience. If we can also see that those who have the power, prestige, and position we lack are, in the last analysis, no happier than us, we achieve an outlook from which our frustrations loom a lot less large.

There are times, no doubt, when utter seriousness and resolute commitment constitute the most appropriate attitude with which to accomplish our aims. Fanaticism is not just an aberration; it is a method of personal unification, of goal-directed behavior. There are other times, however, when wry detachment is more appropriate, for, while it will not win our battles, it can save us from a broken head. Fanaticism, besides, has been the cause of bloodshed and suffering throughout human history, so any device which moderates its excesses deserves consideration on that ground alone.

Our propensity for either attitude, however, is far less practical in intention. We do not choose fanaticism or humor so much as we find ourselves practicing them. Given a certain set of circumstances—sufficient frustration, a need to feel powerful, and a code that promises great things—most of us will hop on the bandwagon. Given another set of circumstances—sufficient frustration, but less desire for power than for peace of mind—many of us will acquire a humorous outlook.

We are apt to identify certain individuals with fanaticism, certain others with humor, and fail to appreciate the fact that both are potentials within every human being. Because of this shortsightedness, we see the struggle for control of fanaticism entirely as a social, interpersonal issue, when in reality it is also a psychological, intrapersonal conflict. If we are convinced that extremism needs to be curbed, we would be well advised to expend some effort discovering the ridiculous side of our own creeds and dogmas—if, indeed, we are not too dense to know they exist.

Fanaticism, at base, is enthralling because it affords us a godlike feeling of superiority. It lures us with the fool's gold of absolute truth and the siren song of self-sacrifice. The glory of upholding, with our very life if necessary, some magnificent cause or shining ideal is as powerful as thunder to a frightened child. Humor, on the face of it, may seem too mild a force to corral such a mighty steed. In its unassuming way, however, it affords us a set of alternatives: not glory but detachment, not power but humility, not victory but acceptance. Its offerings may not glitter, but, like the clear skies after the storm, their peaceful appeal is not without its charm.

Laughter
and
Women's Lib

A set of questions which for centuries was not considered worthy of discussion has in recent years become debatable. Are there any inherent differences between men and women? Aside from the obvious, and always interesting, anatomical distinctions, are the differences we observe inborn or merely learned? Are men innately more aggressive, women more submissive? Are women by nature more emotional and subjective, men more rational and objective? Are men more stable, women more unstable?

The issue, as even such a simple list reveals, is hardly academic. Implicit in these traditional terms of comparison lies the belief that men are *better* creatures than women— more admirable, more reliable, more advanced in human development. The classical identification of masculinity with consciousness, reason, and light, and femininity with unconsciousness, irrationality, and darkness, expresses this distinction succinctly. Since time immemorial, both Western and Eastern civilization have fostered the notion that maleness is preferable to femaleness.

Within the past few decades, however, this presumption has come under increasing attack. Anthropologists have discovered that the character traits the sexes develop are influenced by the expectations of the society in which they are raised. Changing social conditions have shown that, given more freedom of opportunity, women in our own society manifest abilities which were formerly thought to be exclusively masculine. And now the women's liberation movement categorically asserts that all sexual differences are either illusory or learned.

The evidence of history and biology, certain scholars maintain, is being dumped into the trash barrel. The fact that other animal species regularly exhibit sexual differences is ignored, and the opinions of psychologists like Freud and Jung—who never doubted for a moment that the psychological makeup of men and women was fundamentally dissimilar—are scoffed at as outmoded.

Where will it end? What body of data will finally resolve the issue? Of that no expert is certain; but one thing we can state for sure: not here, not in this book. This chapter is guaranteed not to solve this dilemma. Its intention, we may as well admit, is to add fuel to the fire by bringing up an aspect of the problem that has so far been ignored.

Other animals may well exhibit sexual differences, but in itself that does not prove that the same is true of humanity. What makes us peculiarly human are not the traits we share with other creatures but the abilities we as a species alone possess. Language, logic, symbolization, art, science, and culture: these are the attributes in terms of which we must probe the differences between men and women. These and one other: laughter. Our sense of humor, after all, distinguishes us from the other beasts as clearly as any other single feature. Neither reptiles nor crustaceans, marsupials nor any of the lower mammals exercise, as far as we can tell, the faculty of humor. What we laugh at, therefore, and how deep our sense of humor goes, are factors that may generate some light—or heat, at least—on the question of human sexual characteristics.

How, then, do men and women compare in the development of their sense of humor? The recorded facts, as luck would have it, are disjointed and inconclusive. We seem to know little and care less about the entire matter. If we are interested, however, in the controversy over sexual differences, even a paltry amount of data may help to compound our confusion. Let us, therefore, examine the available material.

Professional wits and comics, it has often been observed, are predominantly male. Men also seem more adept at telling funny stories. Do these indicia support the view that men are more advanced in humorous development? Male chauvinists may think so, but female chauvinists will be quick to argue that social opportunity and social expectations, not inherent ability or talent, are the deciding factors in learning to tell jokes either for fun or profit. If we agree, besides, that the ability to tell jokes is a criterion of humor only in a superficial sense, this whole area of dissension becomes fruitless to begin with.

More promising, perhaps, are the developmental data that

have been collected on the subject. It would have been more promising, that is, if such data had ever been collected. Unfortunately, what we actually have are scattered bits and fragments recorded by doting parents, peripatetic teachers, single-minded psychoanalysts, and other unreliable observers. No one, to this date, has systematically investigated the development of humor in the sexes; no one, in fact, has systematically investigated the development of humor in any individual or group.

The mélange of bits and pieces we can put together at this time, however, does contain some interesting probabilities. It seems that in infancy no sex-bound differences in sense of humor can be detected. In childhood, boys begin to show some preference for horseplay, girls for verbal wit, but both boys and girls enjoy absurdity, conundrums, word play, and hostile and off-color humor. In adolescence, both sexes indulge in ribaldry, sick jokes, and topical wit, though boys on the whole may feel freer to enjoy filthy stories while girls are more apt to insist that such stories have a point to make before they will accept them as humor. In adulthood, as in all the previous developmental stages, there is no evidence of one sex having a greater absolute capacity for humor, though there are indications that humorous taste and preference follow the lines of sex role as defined by the society in which we live and the groups with which we identify.

Communities which expect women to be modest, for example, tend to have female members who, in public at least, show distaste for coarse, vulgar wit. Communities which condone greater latitude, in contrast, have many female members who indulge in such wit with gusto.

A few objective studies have yielded the finding that men

are more likely to enjoy aggressive, hostile wit, but the differences are slight and not always in evidence. Other common forms of humor—nonsense, word-play, ribald, topical, and philosophical—have either been left unexamined or have shown no distinction between the sexes.

In an attempt to probe this twilight region, a colleague and I have been conducting studies designed to compare male and female reactions to four kinds of humor: absurd, hostile, sexual, and philosophical. Using college students and older college graduates as subjects, we have had them rate their reactions to a series of jokes. Examples of the material employed are as follows:

Absurd:
Q: How do you get an elephant out of a tub of gelatin?
A: Read the directions on the package.

Hostile:
Advice to the overweight: Want to lose ten pounds of ugly, useless fat? Cut off your head.

Sexual:
Arriving home unexpectedly, a husband finds his wife in bed with another man. "See here," he shouts. "Just what do you think you're doing?"

"You see?" says the wife to the man beside her. "Didn't I tell you he was stupid?"

Philosophical:
I can safely say I have no prejudices. Let a man be black or white, Christian, Jew, or Moslem—it makes no difference to me. All I have to know is that he's a human being. He couldn't be worse.

The preliminary findings, based on about a hundred subjects, are illuminating. No significant differences are shown between the sexes on any of the categories, but both men and women appear to enjoy sexual humor more than humor falling into the other three categories and both men and women rate sexual jokes which put down the other sex as funniest of all. These results suggest that, amongst the college-educated portion of the populace at least, there is less sex-bound difference in humorous taste than is popularly supposed. Ribaldry appears to constitute the richest source of laughter for all, and both males and females appreciate the opportunity to see themselves as "one up" in heterosexual relations.

It is not too farfetched, I believe, to infer that despite the growing freedom of sexual expression in our society, a substantial amount of anxiety still surrounds this area of experience and, despite the increasing assertion of equality between the sexes, we still use heterosexual relations as a power struggle from which each partner seeks to emerge victorious.

To all outward appearances, men have traditionally enjoyed sexual dominance over women. Biologically, the male is equipped to exert his will while the female is built for compliance. Sociologically, our culture has allowed men license it has denied to women. As a result, it is often said, the heterosexual balance has been notably lopsided—tilted in favor of male satisfaction. Our sense of humor should tell us, however, that what appears incontrovertible on the surface inevitably becomes more dubious the closer we examine it.

If we are really frank about our sexual relations, we must confess that, while the male may seem to hold the aces, the female has the final trump to play. By the mere act of withholding her own pleasure, a girl can foil her lover's satisfaction any time she wishes, for the less a man considers himself an animal or a biological machine the more he needs to feel that he has given as well as gotten gratification from the act. Even before that culmination point, indeed, the sexual interchange between two people is an intricate affair which, as often as not, the female is more adept at controlling than the male.

In any case, men—while supposedly the dominant sex—have always felt threatened by and vulnerable to their women. We may not like to admit it, but we know that, with a look or a gesture alone, not to speak of her armamentarium of verbal abuse, our darling can lay us low in an instant. In this predicament, many of us attempt to buttress our self-confidence through humor. Jokes about wives and mothers-in-law, about marriage and sexual relations, serve to help us keep our cool in a situation which is fraught with anxiety below the surface.

A newlywed couple, being driven to their honeymoon cottage by a cab-driver who is not sure of the way, cannot contain their ardor. They begin to make love in the back seat. Seeing a fork in the road ahead, the driver says, "I take the next turn, right?"
"No," replies the groom. "This one's all mine."

Stories such as this give us a fleeting, illusory sense of having the situation well in hand. Our women, we cheerfully delude ourselves, are toys for us to play with, pretty baubles designed for our pleasure. It is a revealing fantasy—infuriating to feminists, but pathetic to the objective observer who perceives the weakness that generates it. Any man who needs to think of women as sexual playthings is surely less than convinced of his own ability to relate to them as human beings. We will all deny that the implication applies to us, but the vast appeal of magazines like *Playboy*, which cater to this very fantasy, indicates that it applies to millions of our brothers. In an enormous number of cases, we must conclude, men have felt insecure about their ability to handle their women and have resorted to wit as a coping device.

How ironic, then, to find that women feel equally insecure about their ability to handle their men. They may be less likely to work it off through laughter, but their frantic consumption of beauty aids alone makes it clear that they labor under as much heterosexual anxiety as their mates.

The women's liberation movement must, I think, be seen in this perspective. Far more than a rational attempt to insist on equality in social opportunity, it represents, for those involved, a holy cause—a crusade designed to subdue the devils they distrust and despise. The strident quality of their proclamations expresses the intensity of their emotions. This intensity is reflected, too, in their reluctance to laugh at themselves and their mission. Proponents of women's lib often utilize scornful wit as a rhetorical device in their diatribes against the chauvinistic male, but good-natured humor about our common inability to appreciate and accept each other is at a minimum in their publications.

"Let's admit it, girls. Men are *superior. Superior at killing, superior at swindling, superior at guzzling beer. It's no use denying it. What's true is true."*

"Sigmund Freud claimed that women suffer from penis envy. But what did he know about it? He ignored his own until he was thirty and sublimated it by the time he was forty." (A reference to the fact that

Freud, who was quite chaste and puritanical in his personal life, married at thirty and ten years later made a remark to the effect that sexual passion was no longer important in his life.)

Caustic remarks like these represent the kind of wit that is at present emanating from the movement. They disclose its great need to disparage the notion of male supremacy and its lack of objectivity with regard to the problem. They are being matched by quips made by men who profess to find the issue amusing.

"Women libbers are okay, I guess—but would you want your sister to marry one?"

"So the women want equal opportunity? Well, they've all got an equal opportunity to get into bed with me."

Here, too, the intent of the jests is disparaging and the joker's bitterness obtrudes. Men who feel a need to ridicule the women's liberation movement may pretend to be detached, but their very compulsion to make wisecracks about it reveals the threat it poses to their security.

Few members of either sex, unfortunately, seem capable of rising above the battle and noting the myriad ironies that pervade the actual scene. Some stories come close to capturing it, but they are scarce and fugitive.

"Yes dear," says a typical suburban husband to his dainty little wife, "I know I've been treating you like my servant all these years. Of course I'm sorry, darling. I agree with you: it's despicable to be a tyrant. Please don't be mad at me. Please."

"Womensh lib," says a drunk to his female companion, "ish a Commie plot to deshtroy the moral fiber of thish great nation!"
"You're damn right!" she replies, waving her glass. "And I say—lesh drink to it!"

For all their grotesque exaggeration, the characters who deliver these lines stand as representative of our species. On the public platform, men and women both may proclaim their independence, their rationality, their fairness and dignity. In those unguarded moments when our secret selves peek out of their crevices, however, we reveal our mutual weakness and our downright foolishness.

On the issue of equality as in every other controversy, we betray our own best interests in the heat of self-assertion. Much as we need to contend with each other, we need even more to accept each other. Our greatest happiness, we know too well, lies in our mutual embrace. When we despair of love and understanding, we may seek power as a substitute, but in our hearts the emptiness remains. In this malaise, our sense of humor, like our sexual drive, can prove a potent remedy. Any couple who have fought all day and made up half the night know the bliss that our fundamental need for each other can engender. What is not so clearly recognized, however, is the warmth that laughter at our shared stupidity can kindle just as well.

Men, surely, have been less than generous in their views and treatment of women. The fair sex, meanwhile, have been something other than fair in their relations with men. If we operate out of our perfectly justified resentment, we may all feel impelled to seek revenge. If we operate out of our sense of humor, however, we may feel more inclined to emulate a certain wise old rabbi.

Consulted by a battling couple to help settle their disputes, he listened first to the wife's complaints. When she had delivered her harangue, he said, "Yes, you're right. You are absolutely right."

Then he let the husband tell his side of the story. When the angry man had finished, he said, "You are right. You are certainly right."

  At this point the rabbi's assistant intervened. "What's wrong with you, rabbi?" he exclaimed. "You know you can't tell two opposing parties that they're both in the right!"

  Regarding him with equanimity, the wise one replied, "Yes, my son. You too are right."

It may win applause from neither the fervent devotees of women's liberation nor from their equally fervent opponents, but, with regard to the issues that antagonize the sexes, this judgment may in the end prove more enduring than any other.

The Genesis
of Humorous
Genius

Humorous genius, like other creative abilities, is best explained as the evolving product of an interplay of forces. To attempt to locate its source in hereditary or environmental factors alone is sophomoric; even the conception of a combination of the two is insufficient. Both nature and nurture are necessary ingredients, of course, but the leavening that induces this particular dough to rise is a matter of identity-formation.

The hereditary base of humorous talent is thought to be demonstrated in families and racial groups whose members exhibit an uncommon aptitude for wittiness and comic behavior. It is equally conceivable, however, that the aptitude is easily learned in such surroundings, simply because it is being displayed on every side. If mother or father indulge in the play of wit, the child who observes their amusement is likely to emulate them. If mother or father delight in cracking jokes, moreover, the child who seeks their approval is likely to feel highly motivated to acquire the knack himself.

Nevertheless, some individuals do seem, from early childhood on, more adept than their siblings and playmates at picking up the skill. If we pursue the possibility of genetic factors influencing these cases, how shall we define them? No one, I suppose, would seriously postulate a specific gene for wit, so we are forced to conceive of an amalgam of mental and emotional features. Alertness in contradistinction to sluggishness, intelligence in the sense of shrewdness, rebelliousness in contrast to cooperativeness, a preference for free-associative rather than conventional thought processes: all these characteristics typify the "natural" comic and may, in some respects, turn out to be innate.

A more important characteristic, however, remains to be considered. Let us call it playfulness: the inclination for fun, for exuberance, for taking things lightly rather than somberly. This quality is possibly more central to humor than any other. Can it be cogently described as running stronger in one family or racial group than another? Probably not. As children, we all exhibit it. What differentiates us in this respect is not how much of it we are born with but what we do with it as we grow up.

What we do with our sense of humor—be it an amalgam of playfulness, alertness, shrewdness, rebelliousness, and free-associative thinking or anything else—is in fact the crucial issue. Even if comic aptitude is as genetically determined as musicality, the man who becomes a full-fledged humorous genius, like the man who becomes a proficient composer, will have labored long and hard to refine, polish, cultivate, and expand his natural gift.

At first, however, it is less appropriate to say that he does it than that he is led to do it. In childhood certainly, and possibly through adolescence, the humorist-in-the-bud is as susceptible to the influence of those around him as the rest of his contemporaries. He may take conscious pleasure in the exercise of his wit, but the incentive to do it at all, the examples of how to do it well, and the rewards for having done it are supplied, in large part, by his environment. If he grows up in a social milieu which is steeped in a humorous tradition, if he is surrounded by friends and relatives who practice the art in their daily lives, if his own comic antics are greeted with enthusiasm, he will be mightily encouraged to parade his humorous talents. If, on the other hand, he is surrounded by glum, dour characters and chastised when he dares to play a joke on them, he is likely to suppress his natural endowment.

This environmental influence, of course, continues in some measure throughout life, but there comes a time in the maturation of the exceptional humorist-to-be when his commitment becomes relatively independent of it. In this period of identity-formation, the future professional decides —sometimes quite consciously, sometimes in a hazy awareness—that he is and will prove himself to be a humorist, no matter what it takes to do so.

Such a decision amounts to much more than a mere wish or intention. It amounts to a milestone in self-identification, a milestone from which he cannot turn back without confusion and a sense of defeat. Having determined on a vocation as a humorist is equivalent, to the man who will make it his life-work, to having perceived himself as an artist. At the moment, his creations may be paltry but, from the day of decision on, a major portion of his attention is

devoted to assimilating the techniques of his craft and cultivating his unique style and approach to it. He becomes consistently, obsessively, attuned to the comedy of everyday life,
he amasses a repertoire of jokes and routines, he studies the
productions of other wits, and he refines his talent until it
becomes an integral part of his being.

Whether he will be successful in the eyes of the world and
whether he will find fulfillment in his chosen profession
remains to be seen, but the fateful step in actualizing himself
as a humorist is taken in the solitude of his inmost self. It is
not, however, unrelated to his other personal needs. While
being blessed with a cluster of qualities which predispose him
to wit and being raised in an environment which encourages
and rewards it are the common underpinnings of humorous
genius, the crucial decision to cast his lot in that direction is
frequently made as a reaction to painful, distressing problems. In line with most other forms of art, humorous creativity affords its creator a means of coping with, and possibly
resolving, conflicts and anxieties arising from his personal life
circumstances and his sensibility to the circumstances of his
contemporaries. In the act of being funny, ironic, or satirical,
the humorist achieves surcease from stress and creates for
himself, as he creates for his audience, islands of tranquility
in the stormy seas of living.

If the principles outlined above are anything more than
airy speculations, they should be apparent in the histories of
well-established humorists. Let us, therefore, review the early
experiences of such a group of men to see how well they
support our contentions regarding the genesis of this particular talent.

SHOLOM ALEICHEM

As the son of a scholarly Jewish merchant in nine-teenth-century Russia, Sholom Aleichem was born into a milieu that appreciated literary humor. Not only did they appreciate it; the intelligent but poverty-stricken, pious, hard-working, oppressed Jews of his time relied on ironic humor as a refuge and resuscitator of their spirits. Other members of his family were not particularly noted as wits or comics, but his father and his father's friends dearly loved a well-told story. That their appreciation influenced the boy in his choice of vocation is apparent in his memory of a certain evening during his early childhood. Some of the leading citizens of the Jewish community had come to his home to celebrate the departure of the Sabbath. His father was read-ing to the guests from a Yiddish book and all were laughing and enjoying themselves. Sholom was still too young to understand what was being read, but "he envied that man who had written that book, and his greatest wish was that, with God's help, he too, when he grew up, would write a book like that, a little book which people would read and laugh at. . . ."

In a letter to a friend, he once recalled, "To notice and point up the ludicrous in everything and everyone—this was almost a sickness with me. Unthinkingly I used to mimic everybody, my teacher Reb Zorach, his wife, the other pupils, their fathers and mothers, even Baruch Ber, the drunkard, and the Gentile janitor with his crooked legs. I used to get many slaps for this. At the *cheder* I was the comic. Everyone used to laugh, laugh until they cried . . ."

The occasion of Sholom Aleichem's first literary effort seems highly significant for his future career. A young adolescent, he was subject to the verbal abuse and harassment of his stepmother, a woman who rarely spared the sensibilities of her many stepchildren. According to all accounts, she frequently beat them, starved them, and cursed them in the classic manner. As a means, we may infer, of coping with the feelings this treatment must have aroused in him, Sholom began to compose a lexicon of abusive terms, which he entitled "The Glib Tongue of a Stepmother." The entries included such epithets as "ass; alley cat; bedbug; bellyache; diddler; glutton; worthless one; runny nose," etc. One day his father happened upon the work and, to the boy's dismay, decided to read it to the stepmother herself. Instead of the expected rebuke, however, Sholom found them laughing and enjoying it immensely.

Without stretching the factual evidence, we may, I think, conclude that Sholom Aleichem, the boy who was to become the greatest Jewish humorist of all time, possessed a natural comic talent that was nurtured and encouraged by his childhood environment. He employed it very early as a means of gaining attention and, more interestingly, as an outlet for feelings evoked by the oppressive tactics of his stepmother. When his wit was received with mirth, not only by his playmates but by his respected father and, surprisingly enough, by the feared and resented target of his scorn, his vocation was all but determined. By the time he was a young man, Sholom Aleichem had clearly identified himself as a humorist. The rest of his long and productive life was spent in expanding, deepening, and validating this identification.

RICHARD ARMOUR

Though he has published over forty books of light verse and gentle satire, Richard Armour was, in his own words, "not above average in the wit department as a child." Both his father and his uncle, however, were notably witty, and he himself began to write humorous pieces in college.

He did not commit himself to a career as a humorist until some years after he had taken his Ph.D. at Harvard. "I remember the summer of 1937, when my wife had gone to visit her relatives in California and I was left alone in the little college town of Aurora-on-Cayuga in upstate New York. Perhaps it was being alone and needing something to do. For whatever reason, I wrote two pieces of light verse and sold one to *The Saturday Evening Post* and the other to *The New Yorker*. This I know: once I had placed these first pieces in widely read magazines, I was committed, or stuck. I have written every day, almost without exception, ever since."

Four facts which are pertinent to our inquiry emerge from these reminiscences. First, Armour's father and uncle provided models with which the boy could identify and, by their example, encouraged expression of humorous talent. Second, Armour's keen and perceptive wit was not in evidence until his late teens. Third, his first serious literary venture along these lines was undertaken as a means of coping with a period of loneliness. And most important, once his initial efforts had been crowned with success, he dedicated himself unswervingly to the vocation of humorous writing.

STEVE ALLEN

The popular celebrity whose genial wit has entertained millions of television viewers, Steve Allen has been described as "probably as funny at age five as he was ever to become." He was the class clown in grammar school, the neighborhood prankster, and the practical joker and comic of his adolescent peer group.

"I came from a family of fast-talking, sarcastic Irish wits," he has said. "My mother, Belle Montrose, was a vaudeville comedienne. Milton Berle calls her the funniest woman in vaudeville."

His father having died when Steve was eighteen months of age, he was raised by his mother and her relatives. He recalls many times when he watched her perform; as a matter of fact, he remembers her entire routine verbatim to this day.

She was forced to leave him, however, for months at a time while she was on the road. During these periods he was boarded out with a succession of aunts, uncles, grandmothers, and strangers. When his mother decided to take him with her, the conditions were not much more comforting. He would frequently wake up alone in strange hotel rooms and wander out to search for her. Their relationship, he has written, was "a little like certain marriages of which people say, 'I can't live with her and I can't live without her.'"

Nevertheless, he grew up to follow in her footsteps insofar as he has made comedy his stock in trade. If she was in fact the funniest woman in vaudeville, her son is surely one of the most talented humorists on television.

Allen exercised his comic inclinations from childhood on, wrote a humor column in his college newspaper, took a job as a radio announcer in Phoenix and enlivened the program with his wit, moved to Los Angeles and more and more successful radio comedy, and was well on his way to national acclaim by the time he was twenty-five.

For the purposes of our discussion, we may note that an unusual comic strain seems to run in his family; that his mother provided a prime example of comedy as a vocation; that his natural talent was abetted by various relatives; that the loneliness and dislocations he experienced as a child must have given him an intense need to belong—to belong to his mother and her family, which he could most readily achieve by identifying with their behavior, and to belong to the people of the world, which he has achieved by becoming an amusing, cheerful, cordial entertainer; and especially, that he perceived his talent early and lost little time in turning it into a highly successful professional career.

While obviously anecdotal and incomplete, these casual case histories will serve to illustrate our thesis. They suggest that the professional humorist is likely to have grown up in a witty family (there is evidence of this in all three cases); that he is likely, but not certain, to have shown comic talent in childhood (Sholom Aleichem and Steve Allen did; Richard Armour did not); that his humor is likely to have served him as a means of coping with personal stress (Sholom Aleichem's lexicon of his stepmother's curses; Richard Armour's writing during a period of loneliness; Steve Allen's identification with his peripatetic mother); and finally, that, having once identified himself as a humorist and having been recognized as such, he is likely to remain completely dedicated to his calling for the rest of his life (all three have done so).

The genesis of humorous genius is not, to be sure, conclusively explained by this body of data, but some steps toward its explanation have been taken. Systematic investigation could advance, enlarge upon, or modify these steps by studying the formative years of a much larger group of humorists in much greater detail.

We are left, however, with an important question that has not been touched upon. Given the capacity and conditions for becoming a professional humorist, why does each man create his own unique brand of wit? What, in other words, determines any given style? This question is equivalent to asking why, among playwrights, one produces melodrama and another theater of the absurd, or why, among artists, one paints rigid realism and another slapdash expressionism.

The answer, common sense suggests, must lie in a combination of personal need and social receptivity. The comic who specializes in hostile, insulting wit probably does so, in part, because he needs this kind of outlet and, in part, because his audience appreciates it. The humorist who excels in nonsense probably derives particular gratification from confounding reason while he also supplies an experience his audience enjoys.

Creative persons—be they artists, scientists, or humorists— often object to psychological investigation of their talents. When the investigation is conducted dogmatically and results in nothing more than a description of the subjects' neuroses, their objections are well taken. If the investigation, on the other hand, provides real understanding of the inner and outer forces that give rise to creative achievements, its justification is incontestible.

The relationship between the humorist's public image and his private self; the relationship between the kind of humor he purveys and the needs and expectations of his audience: these issues, pursued in careful study of many individual cases, could provide a fascinating account of the development of humorous genius and, in the process, afford a glimpse into the dynamics of creativity.

Humor
as
Therapy

Catharsis, insight, self-acceptance, reconditioning, and emotional openness: these experiences, by and large, have been the classical agents of psychotherapy. By fostering one or more of them, psychologists and psychiatrists have attempted—and sometimes even managed—to help their patients cope with their distress. The field, however, has been limited to variations on these themes. It is time, therefore, to propose an addition to their ranks. In these days, in particular, when clinical inspiration is restricted to the ecstasies of the existentialists and the banalities of the behaviorists, we are ripe for a new therapeutic gambit. We stand in need of an agent that can help us when the traditional forms of treatment falter.

Such an agent exists. It has, in fact, been part of our human equipment since time immemorial. Its name—no

joke—is humor. Humor not in its superficial, merely entertaining manifestations, but in its deepest, most genuine
essence. We all agree that when a person—patient, therapist,
or normal human being—exercises this faculty, he becomes
more resilient to the stresses of living. What we need to
understand, however, is the process by which the faculty can
be brought into play and, for those in the business, the role
the psychotherapist can perform in activating it.

Let us be clear now on what we are talking about. Humor
in its deepest essence: what does the phrase denote? Is it the
ability to tell jokes and make people laugh? No. Delightful as
they may be, jokes and comic routines are contrived, artificial products. They bear about the same relation to
genuine humor as painting pretty pictures does to art. Is it
then the ability to deliver spontaneous witticisms? Not quite.
Such a talent comes closer to humor's core, but it does not
encompass it. Deep, genuine humor—the humor that deserves
to be called therapeutic, that can be instrumental in our
lives—extends beyond jokes, beyond wit, beyond laughter
itself to a peculiar frame of mind. It is an inner condition, a
stance, a point of view, or in the largest sense an attitude to
life.

A cluster of qualities characterize it. Flexibility, spontaneity, unconventionality combined with shrewdness, playfulness, and humility: they each play their part in the drama of
the humorous outlook. For that drama to unfold, therefore,
each one of these qualities must be called upon. The starring
role, however, is reserved for a specific characteristic. We may
call it enjoyment of the ironies that run through all human
affairs. To command a deep sense of humor, a person must
become acutely, vividly, aware of the anomalies and paradoxes that embroider our behavior. He must come to know,

not theoretically but practically, with all his being, that the happiest relationships are larded with suffering, that the greatest accomplishments are anticlimactic, that rational acts are motivated by irrational drives, that psychotic thinking makes excellent sense, that the most altruistic gestures are selfish at their core. He must know these things and enjoy them—enjoy them because they are true and because they give three, if not four, dimensions to human beings.

The peculiarities of our characters make us the infuriating, fascinating creatures we are. It is not by accident that man is the only animal who has a sense of humor. He is also the only animal who wears clothing, denies himself sex, worships nonexistent deities, starves in order to create, kills and dies for his country, slaves and cheats for his bank balance. Clearly, he is the only animal who *needs* a sense of humor.

An ancient folk tale illustrates these observations succinctly. It tells of a morose young man who met a kind fairy in the woods.

"What ails thee?" asked the fairy.

"I would be happy," the young man replied, "if only I were handsome."

So the fairy instructed him in the application of certain salves and ointments, and lo and behold, in a short while the young man was very handsome.

He remained, however, despondent. Once again the fairy asked, "What ails thee?"

"I would be happy," said the handsome young man, "if only I were rich."

So the fairy taught him how to find precious jewels in hidden caves in the mountains, and in no time at all the young man became exceedingly wealthy.

He remained, nevertheless, downcast. And yet again the fairy asked, "What ails thee?"

"I would be happy," said the rich and handsome young man, "if only I were loved."

*So the fairy introduced him to the subtle art of winning fair maidens'
affections, and soon he was well beloved by many charming girls.
Despite his success, however, he remained dejected. One last time,
therefore, the fairy inquired, "What ails thee?"*

*And the rich and handsome and well beloved young man replied, "I
would be happy, really happy, if only I had something to strive for."*

Like the hero of this simple tale, we are all more impossible than we acknowledge. We yearn for whatever we do not
have and, when allowed to do everything exactly as we wish,
we end up painting ourselves into corners. We make life
difficult for ourselves and we make it difficult for each other.
Consider the cartoon on the following page.

One way or another, we are both the perpetrators and the
victims of this kind of maneuver. We create, for ourselves and
others, intolerable predicaments from which there is no
escape. Life can be pleasant, we all know that; but somehow
or other we always manage to screw it up. That, in short, is
the vein of truth that genuine humor mines. What makes it a
liberating rather than a depressing discovery, however, is the
particular manner in which it is unearthed. To our sense of
humor, even the brutal truth is curious, a source of amusement, because we are not completely identified with it. We
see our irrationality, our stupidity, our immorality as facts of
life but not the ultimate facts, for infuriating as we may be,
we know that we are also lovable, and ridiculous as we may
behave, we know that we are also sensible.

When we operate out of our sense of humor, we train a
widened perspective on ourselves. We see ourselves and our
lives from a certain distance, and that distance makes all the
difference in the world. Several years ago, I had a dream that
opened my eyes to this perspective. It came at a time when I

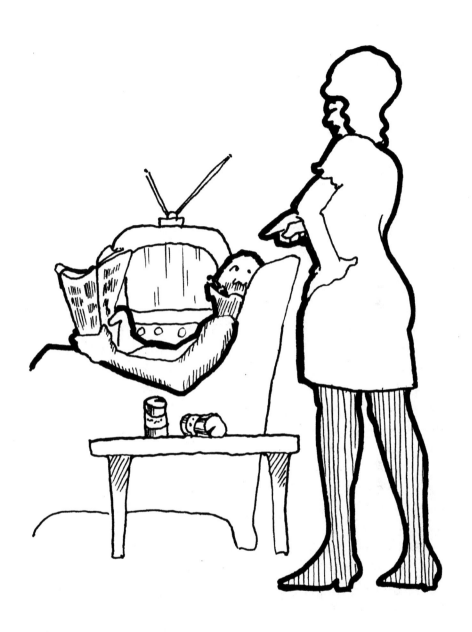

"What's wrong with you is—you can't take criticism."

was feeling unusually defeated; whatever was most important to me was going wrong and I could visualize no way to remedy my situation. In the dream, I heard a voice speak to me. It was a cool, impersonal voice, and all it said was, "One day you were born, one day you will die." Now that may not seem like a very funny observation, but it lightened my spirits considerably. It articulated a view from which all my troubles looked much less calamitous, and it is precisely that kind of view that a deep sense of humor promotes.

If my description is apt, if the suggestion that genuine humor involves both a widened perspective on ourselves and an appreciation of the ironies on which our lives are built is to the point, the question that faces me as a psychotherapist is: how can I encourage it in my patients? My dream may have evoked it for a time in me, but how can I evoke it in that troubled person pouring out his heart to me?

Directly? No. I am convinced of that because, whenever I am feeling troubled, my friends are apt to say, "Well, you're the big humor expert. Why don't you laugh it off?"—a piece of advice that rarely pastes a smile on my face. No; as with love or faith or courage, it avails little to *advise* a patient to exercise his sense of humor. I might just as well write out a prescription—"One teaspoonful of wit before every meal and at bedtime"—for all the good it will do.

Nor does it do much good to try to make a patient laugh. It might be possible, for a therapist whose wit was sharp enough, to ridicule or chide his patients into seeing the ludicrous side of their complaints, but I doubt that his efforts would be appreciated. More than likely, he would receive a few wallops for his trouble, which might make the whole procedure more comical to the onlooker but which would hardly win him the analyst-of-the-year award.*

The problem is, to say the least, perplexing. How does one encourage an outlook which, to be genuine, must be spontaneous? It seems like a contradiction in terms, and yet it is precisely such contradictions on which humor thrives. From personal experience, I think it can be done, and I even think I can indicate how. The process is analogous to growing plants or flowers, in the sense that we can provide the conditions conducive to their growth, though it would be folly to grab them by the stems and try to yank them up.

The conditions conducive to the growth of genuine humor are those I mentioned earlier. Flexibility: in this case, a willingness to examine every side of every issue and every

---

* Since writing this chapter, I have changed my mind on this score. I have become so bold that I have tried, now and then, to "kid" a patient out of his or her desperation, and the reactions have not all been negative. Once, for example, a woman I had been seeing for several months threatened to commit suicide. She had made some messy and abortive suicidal gestures in the past, so now, when she wailed that her life was so miserable that she thought she might kill herself, I said, "Oh yeah. That's the great solution you came up with before!" and, instead of telling me to go to hell, she laughed, saw her foolishness and relinquished that particular gambit—at least for that particular day.

But it is a risky game to make fun of someone else's anguish, even with the best of intentions. You can never be sure your humor won't be interpreted as derision. In fact, you can be sure it will—unless, and this is the key, the patient unequivocally perceives you as his or her ally. The safest course, I think, is to watch for any sign that the patient himself has an inkling of the ridiculousness of his behavior or the irony of his predicament and then jump in and reinforce it by agreeing with him and praising him for seeing it that way.

side of every side. Spontaneity: the ability to leap instanta-
neously from one mood or mode of thought to another.
Unconventionality: freedom from the values of time, place,
and even profession. Shrewdness: the refusal to believe that
anyone—least of all one's self—is what he seems to be. Playfulness: the grasp of life as a game, a tragicomic game which
nobody wins but which does not have to be won to be
enjoyed. And humility: that elusive simpleness that disappears whenever we are conscious of having attained it.

The point is that to encourage a humorous outlook in his
patients the therapist must keep the dimension alive in himself. If he can perceive the irony in their predicaments and in
his own as well, his perception will permeate his interviews
and will, when his patients are supple enough to take it,
enlarge their comprehension of themselves.

But there—I'm afraid we must confess—'s the rub. A glance
at any professional journal, a visit to any professional meet-
ing, make it apparent that psychotherapists take themselves
too seriously. We really believe—and the more renowned
among us believe it the more—that the theories we propound
and the techniques we apply are cogent, valid, and beneficial.
Not only *do* we believe it; we *must* believe it to be effective.
And yet, as long as the belief is maintained, a deep and
genuine sense of humor cannot be achieved and therefore
promoted. As long as we fail to contemplate the likelihood
that our professional activities are useless, that psychotherapy of any sort is absurd in the larger scale of things, we
remain bound to the very outlook from which we need to
free our patients.

We could do worse than take a cue from a former patient
of mine. An attractive, intelligent young woman, she was

suffering from obesity. She had tried every method of reducing but had had no success to speak of. One day, however, she composed the following paragraphs. They did not, let me hasten to add, enable her immediately to lose weight, but they did, I believe, mark the opening of a new perspective on her plight:

"*I just got the most beautiful insight about how to solve a vexing social problem in what I might modestly term a completely original way. It is simply to make being obese against the law. My thinking or it is this. Many things in this world are exceedingly tempting, but society has coped by making them illegal. Other people's wives, property, possessions, little goodies like these have tempted malefactors through the ages. How to discourage them? Everything from social ostracism to capital punishment has been tried to more or less effect. In this light it is clear to me and to others of my ilk, or should I say bulk, that some motivation beyond self-disgust and the oy-veys of husband and family must become operational. You take your average chubby housewife who has caught a nice husband and is raising a family and coping with Life. She often eats as an outlet, less dangerous to everyone's well-being than, say, flirting with the Helm's man or sniffing glue with the high-school dropout across the street. But now this can change. If you confront her with the prospect of being hauled into court on an obesity charge, sentenced by a judge and fined or imprisoned, I think you would be well on your way to a permanent solution of this disgraceful problem. But why should such drastic measures be applied to these unfortunates, you may be asking. Well, fat people take up too much of the earth's precious room and air, they crowd you on the bus and they crush you on the elevator, and for their own good they have to take the strain off their feet, their hearts, and their consciences.*

"*In case you're wondering, yes, this is a personal problem. I admit I'm desperate. I've tried everything, now I'm yelling for help. The government has stepped in everywhere else, so why not here? Please. Somebody! Stop me before I eat again. Where is the relentless arm of the law? Where are the measures for girth control? All interested senators and congressmen please contact me. I can usually be found in the back booth of Kantor's Delicatessen. Just look for a large, guilty-looking woman eating an Eddie Cantor Special (turkey, ham, roast beef, and chopped liver on rye).*"

When a person begins to see his own predicament in a humorous light, he is on his way to overcoming it. Not necessarily to eliminating it—our central dilemmas, we must know by now, can never be eliminated anyway—but to overcoming its debilitating influence on his well-being.

Because it raises us above our usual level of comprehension and allows us to accept what would ordinarily be unacceptable, spontaneous, genuine humor is a coping mechanism of the very highest caliber. It should, therefore, be one of the psychotherapist's goals to further its development. He is, in fact, in an excellent position to do so, since his own calling is nothing if not ridiculous. Every day of his life, patients come to him expecting what he cannot give but must give, so that, in the process, they can discover in themselves what they mistakenly, but necessarily, had hoped he possessed.

In the framework of such an admittedly ironic outlook, I have tried to indicate how humor can be cultivated in psychotherapy. My suggestions themselves may seem a joke. Perhaps they are. But if so—in all seriousness—I don't think that would be so bad.

The Psychology
of Jokes
on Psychology

Psychotherapy, in the last few decades, has become a prime target for wit. Despite, or perhaps because of, the gravity of the problems with which it deals, it has taken its place with sex and religion as one of our culture's favorite butts. Cartoonists, comics, and the joker-in-the-street all join in the fun of making light of the profession, and no practitioner is spared their humorous barbs.

The jokes engendered by psychotherapy are numerous, but their themes are not at all haphazard. They dwell on distinctive features of the field and express distinctive reactions to it. Both defensive and perceptive, they reveal, on the one hand, the threat the profession poses to the populace at large and, on the other, its shortcomings as seen by the disenchanted layman.

If we take time to examine a sampling of this family of

jests, we may salvage more than a chuckle for our efforts.

A psychiatrist, working in a mental hospital, determined to cure a patient of the delusion that he had become a zombie. He would, he decided, prove to him that the idea was ridiculous.

"Listen," he began. "How can you be a zombie? You're walking and talking, aren't you?"

"Zombies walk and talk," the patient muttered.

"Well then, you're breathing, aren't you?"

"Zombies breathe," the patient replied.

"All right," said the psychiatrist. "There must be something zombies don't do. Tell me, do zombies bleed?"

"No," said the patient. "Zombies do not bleed."

"Great!" The doctor was elated. "Then I am going to stick this needle into your arm, and we'll soon see if you are suffering from a delusion or not."

Accordingly, he pierced the patient's arm and the blood began to flow profusely. The patient stared at it in horrified disbelief. Then, shamefaced, he conceded, "I was wrong. Zombies do bleed."

This story sounds one movement in the concerto of jokes on psychology. Sketches, quips, and anecdotes within this movement take various paths, but they all arrive at the same destination: somehow or other, in every one of them, insanity or absurdity prevails over reason.

A lady visits an analyst to discuss her husband's problem.

"It's terrible," she says. "He thinks he's a horse. He lives in a stable, he walks on all fours, and he even eats hay. Please tell me, doctor—can you cure him?"

"Yes, I believe I can," says the analyst. "But I have to warn you, the treatment will be long and expensive."

"Oh, money's no object," the lady replies. "He's already won two races."

The theme is not new. It has been echoed and reechoed ever since psychotherapy began. Many a cartoon, for instance, has depicted a patient complaining that everyone she sees looks like a rabbit or a beetle or a head of lettuce, and in each such cartoon her therapist closely resembles a rabbit or a beetle or a head of lettuce. The gist of all these jokes resides precisely in the triumph of the irrational. Insanity or kookiness is made victorious over reality, and the victory unfailingly tickles our funnybone.

Connoisseurs of humor may advance the observation that this principle is not confined to jokes on psychology. Throughout history, nonsense humor has amused people by confounding their reasoning faculties. The contention is certainly true. This line of psychological wit is just a special case of nonsense wit in general. Let us pause, then, to consider two pertinent questions. Why is the theme a perennial favorite? And why does it work so well in the framework of psychotherapy?

The answers are fairly obvious. We all engage in a lifelong conflict between our reasoning powers and our irrationality, a struggle we regularly try to resolve in favor of reason. Psychotherapy, by its very nature, suggests and represents this struggle. In our sober, serious hours we commit ourselves to its goal—to the goal of accepting reality—but within us lurks the renegade. Convinced as we may be of the necessity for sanity, we retain nostalgic yearnings for the magic world of childhood. Nonsense jokes in general, and nonsense jokes refuting psychotherapy in particular, allow this world an airing. They delight that part of us that needs to cling to its pet delusions, and the pleasure they evoke reveals how vital that part really is.

The tournament of wit versus reason, however, applies primarily to traditional forms of therapy. Some newer techniques, as we all know, do not encourage a submission to rationality. On the contrary, the existential, encounter-group approach insists on a submission *of* rationality to emotional, sensory, gut-level kinds of experience and the behaviorist approach eschews both rational insight and emotional expression in favor of re-conditioning unwanted behavior patterns. It is intriguing, then, to see what happens to humor. Deprived of its familiar target, must it retreat from the field? Hardly. The emergence of newer forms of therapy simply provide it with fresh, fat butts to ridicule.

"Okay group," proclaims one encounter therapist, "we're going to keep practicing spontaneity until we get it right!"

A participant in a nude therapy session, assaying a luscious chick, slyly whispers to his pal, "Man, I'd like to see her *in a bikini."*

On the other side of the ledger, one behavior therapist admonishes a teary housewife, "Forget about love. The secret of marital happiness lies in control of the vaginal muscles," while another confidently asserts, "Just follow our schedules of reinforcement, beep beep, and you'll become as well-adjusted as I am, click whirr beep click click."

With his beard and straggly hair, his sandals and open shirt, his swinging manner and turned-on style, the "hip" psychologist may be as easy to satirize as the man behind the couch, but the robot-worshipping behaviorist who guilelessly dreams of the day when therapy will be conducted by computers stands as a parody on himself.

Satirization and parody of the practitioner is the primary business of jokes on psychotherapy. Before we discuss it further, however, let us survey its subsidiary enterprises. A minor, but interesting topic of psychological humor is the jargon of the field. "Oedipus shmedipus—as long as he loves his mother" may be the classic line in this area, but it is matched by the inscription on the wall of the ancient Greek lavatory—"Oedipus is a motherfucker"—and, in another vein, the sketch of a courtroom scene in which the defense attorney says, "Your honor, my client wishes to plead a castration complex, negative conditioning, and rejection by his peer group."

Whereas the jargon, in jests like these, may be bandied about by anyone, a more wicked batch of psychological jokes makes specific fun of the therapy patient.

Postcard message from a patient to his analyst. "Dear doctor, Having a wonderful time. Wish you were here to tell me why."

Cartoon of a patient clutching his therapist's hand and imploring, "Please tell me, Doctor Smith, have I overcome my dependency?"

We enjoy such quips, it seems, for the sense of superiority they give us. Discovering a person so identified with the role of patient that he cannot shake it off, we imagine ourselves more sensible in comparison. It is significant, however, that we will also laugh at a suggestion of the opposite extreme.

A patient terminating treatment points a gun at his psychiatrist and says, "You've helped me, doc—but now you know too much."

The patient behaving surprisingly out of character is just as funny as the patient behaving too stringently in character. This seeming paradox reflects a basic principle of humor: both incongruity and redundancy are laughable. The image of a Jewish cowboy—a gun-toting, bowlegged fellow sporting a yarmulke and drawling, "Hitch up de veggons, podneh, ve gonna titch dem fellas vots vot"—strikes us as ludicrous because of its incongruity, but, because of its redundancy, we are also inclined to smile at the image of a supercowboy—a lanky guy wearing not a ten-gallon hat but a twenty-gallon hat and not merely drawling his words but drawling his drawl.

An inference we might be tempted to make is that humor as a social agent has a normalizing effect. Since it derides both eccentricity and conformity, it would seem to encourage us to avoid both extremes. Such an inference is only partly justified, however, for it fails to take account of the varying emotions that inform our laughter. The man who writes his analyst, "Having a wonderful time. Wish you were here to tell me why," seems a fool, and we laugh at him with contempt; the one who says, "Now you know too much," in contrast, seems human, all too human, and we laugh at him with envy. In failing to act as a patient should, he betrays his truer self and we admire him for doing so. We all share a need to cast off our conforming habits, however therapeutic they may be, and settle back into our individual flesh and bones. When a joke depicts a person doing exactly that, we chuckle not at his inability to play the social game but at his appealing, unlettered candor.

The same considerations apply in the case of the therapist. One body of jokes portrays him as identified with his professional role, and in these he comes off an idiot. We all know the old one about the two analysts who rode up to work every morning in the same elevator:

As the one who got off first was about to leave, he invariably turned around and spat in his colleague's face. This procedure was repeated day after day, until the elevator operator couldn't stand it anymore. So he said to the second analyst, "Doctor, every morning that guy spits in

your face and you just let him. Why don't you do something about it?"
And the analyst, of course, replied, "Why should I? It's his problem,
isn't it?"

In stories such as this, the therapist is depicted as a jerk.

Another stream of jokes, however, has him behaving surprisingly naturally, and in these he impresses us as having more sense or guts than we gave him credit for. More than one cartoon, for example, shows him smacking or kicking his patient and shouting, "Maybe this'll teach you!" or some variation thereof. In laughing at these, we do not look down on him with contempt but identify with him in fantasy—much as we identify with Groucho Marx and other comic figures who flout conventionality and act out their raw impulses.

We know full well, of course, that both the analyst who says, "It's his problem, isn't it?" and the one who hits his patients are exaggerated caricatures. We ourselves, in our daily lives, may strive to avoid both extremes. The point to note, however, is that if we had to veer one way or the other, we would all prefer to incline toward the latter model. Every one of us suffers from being constrained by his social roles and harbors uncivilized impulses he would love to act out. Our sense of humor simply capitalizes on these universal conditions.

The therapist may come away unscathed or even enviable in a few scattered stories and sketches. The vast majority of jokes on psychology, nevertheless, have one particular purpose: to lambaste the clinician and show him up as a fraud.

"Doctor, I must compliment you," says a patient. "Sitting here hour after hour, day after day, listening to people's endless complaints. You must have the patience of a saint. Tell me, please, how do you do it?"
And the therapist replies with a snore.

"*I will see you Mondays, Wednesdays, and Fridays at three,*" *says the psychiatrist to his new patient,* "*and I advise you to be on time because, if you're not, I start without you.*"

"*Yes, Mother,*" *says the analyst into the telephone.* "*Of course, Mother. Right, Mother. Anything you say, Mother.*"

A cartoonist, meanwhile, draws a therapist consulting his wristwatch to see how much of the hour has elapsed. His watch face, however, is marked off not in minutes but in dollars.

Then again there is the story about the man who consults a psychologist because of kleptomania. After six months of treatment, he seems cured and they decide to terminate. As the patient is leaving, his therapist says, "*It's been very gratifying to work with you, Mr. Brown. Good luck. But if you should ever have a relapse, remember—I can always use a Mixmaster.*"

While this is going on, an analyst is conducting his final interview with a beautiful young woman. She murmurs, "*Doctor, I don't know how to thank you. You've done so much for me. This being our last visit, and just to show my appreciation, don't you think I could kiss you goodbye?*"
"*Oh no, my dear,*" *he replies.* "*That's against the rules of psychoanalysis. As a matter of fact, I've already stretched a point by lying here on the couch with you.*"

And finally there is the one about the man who has been in treatment for ten years. His therapist decides it is time to stop, but the patient is very anxious, so he offers to let him call him in an emergency.
Next morning at six A.M., the psychologist receives a call. "*I had a terrible nightmare,*" *the patient reports.* "*I dreamed you were my mother.*"
"*So what did you do?*"
"*I got up like you taught me and tried to figure it out.*"
"*And what happened?*"
"*While I was figuring it out, I made myself some breakfast.*"
"*Okay. What did you make?*"
"*A cup of coffee.*"
"*A cup of coffee? You call that a breakfast?!!*"

In short order, now, we have seen the psychotherapist depicted as a crook, a mama's boy, a lecher, and a contributor to his patients' problems. Jokes such as these suggest that, for all his training, all his erudition, he is nothing but a sleazy, neurotic character. And what can he reply? Must he, like his patients, take it lying down, or can he strike back in self-defense?

Anyone who knows clinicians should be able to guess. Their bastions are built strong. They block every thrust with ease and counterattack with overwhelming force. In response to the gibes of the jokesters, they calmly reach down into their bag of theories and come up with a thesis:

Wit is a means of attacking a person or a group the joker fears. Perceiving someone as a threat, the humorist makes fun of him in an attempt to reduce his stature. Witty exposure of the therapist's supposed faults, then, is merely evidence of the discomfort he arouses in the populace at large. Standing, as he does, for emotional candor, for penetrating insight, for investigation of all hidden desires, he provokes anxiety wherever he turns. Who will deny his trepidation over what might be revealed were psychotherapy to cast its evil eye on him?

This is the first blow the clinician lands in defense of his honor. "You laugh at us because you fear us." Ha! Take that!

Then comes the uppercut. Wit also involves a wish-fulfillment process. What one ridicules in others is precisely what one wishes for oneself. Quips aimed at the therapist by the layman simply express his envy. They tell us what he secretly yearns for. To defraud and get away with it, to be indifferent to other people's suffering, to sneak erotic pleasures on the sly: who can pretend he isn't tempted? "What you satirize in us is really in yourself." That's the knockout punch. The fight is over. Psychotherapy has won again!

Or has it? When the joker's motivation is revealed, has the last word actually been said? Or could there be some cogency in humor? Could it, perhaps, be true that therapists are laughable, that their behavior is ridiculous? Could it be true that they are just the kinds of hypocrites on whom wit thrives and flourishes?

No, no, of course not! After all, they've all been analyzed, encountered, or re-conditioned as the particular case may be. Mature and authentic, transparent and re-inforced, they have no more need for hypocrisy than they have for self-aggrandizement. But now a doubt creeps in. Is it the therapist's devotion to his patients' welfare, it hisses, that leads him to charge the fees he does? Is it his disinterest in erotic titillation that encourages him to dwell on his patients' sexual behavior and exploit their transference reactions to himself? If it is, the doubt suggests, then he is surely more than human. A paragon of virtue, he deserves to be enshrined with all those other noble souls—doctors, teachers, government officials, ministers, mothers-in-law, and drunks—whose role as traditional butts for laughter is based on nothing substantially flawed in their characters, but merely on the public's misguided envy of their status.

Impaled on the doubt, the therapist shudders visibly. The ghost of his theories takes shape within his mind, intoning all the holy words. "Resistance! Resentment! Projection!" The ghost of his growing uncertainty rises up to contend with it. "Hypocrisy! Lechery! Greed!" What is there to say? What can he do? Distracted, he ransacks his soul for wisdom, for some potent remedy to set the matter right. But what great insight can effect a cure? He ponders, he probes, he quivers in distress. He stares, he swears, he sighs, he cries—then out of his whirling confusion a half-forgotten joke appears:

The analyst, it says, got tired of sitting behind the couch all day, uttering hardly a word, just listening and listening to his patients' flow of thought. So he bought himself a tape recorder and, every morning from ten to ten-thirty, surreptitiously switched it on and slipped downstairs for a cup of coffee.

All went well until one day when whom does he see across the counter but the patient who should have been up in his office spilling out his guts.

"What are you doing here?" the analyst demands. "Isn't this your hour?"

"Yes," the patient replies. "But don't you worry. Everything's okay. Upstairs in the office, you see, my tape recorder is talking to your tape recorder."

The therapist heaves a sigh of relief. His conflict is resolved. He can relax now and enjoy the jokes being told about his specialty, for whatever they imply, in the light of this story he can take it. "*C'est la vie,*" he muses contentedly. "It takes one to catch one."

Section
Three

Appendix

The foregoing study is based on the thesis that humor is an agent of psychological liberation. Since we were able to include every kind of wit and humor under the umbrella of this thesis, it amounts to an informal but comprehensive theory of the ludicrous. Briefly put, the theory proposes that the most fundamental, most important function of humor is its power to release us from the many inhibitions and restrictions under which we live our daily lives.

Other theses, of course, have been propounded in the past. The most ingenious and persuasive of all have been the incongruity and degradation theories: two seemingly unrelated lines of thought, each of which has been employed to explain the essential core of humor.

Two centuries ago, Kant made the observation that laughter is "an affection arising from the sudden transformation of a strained expectation into nothing." The insight contained in this phrase was later expanded, mainly by Schopenhauer, into the incongruity theory of humor. To state it simply, according to this viewpoint laughter is evoked whenever we are led to expect one image or idea and then are suddenly presented with another.

The standard form of the joke, that common vehicle of laughter, illustrates it clearly. Jokes almost always lead us along one avenue of thought and then, with the twist or the punch line, jolt us out of it. Consider the story we briefly discussed in our first chapter (page 22):

Three men lay dying on a hospital ward. Their doctor, making rounds, went up to the first and asked him his last wish. The patient was a Catholic. "My last wish," he murmured, "is to see a priest and make confession." The doctor assured him he would arrange it, and moved on. The second patient was a Protestant. When asked his last wish, he replied, "My last wish is to see my family and say goodbye." The doctor promised he would have them brought, and moved on again. The third patient was, of course, a Jew. "And what is your last wish?" the doctor asked. "My last wish," came the feeble, hoarse reply, "is to see another doctor."

Here the rendering of incongruity is patent. In the solemn setting of life's final ebb, we are led along conventional lines of thought—to make confession, to take leave of one's loved ones—and then jerked round to consider a new outlook altogether. Our expectations have, without a doubt, been tricked; Kant and Schopenhauer would appear to have hit the nail on the head.

Or have they? Even as we pay them their due, can we fail to perceive the fact that the new outlook expressed by the Jewish patient is not entirely incongrous at all? It is unexpected, unconventional, and impolite, but in the end it may prove more congruent, make more sense, than the supposedly sensible requests. Had the patient said, "My last wish is to bake an apple pie," or better, "Googley-googley-glump-glump," his response would have been more completely incongrous but not nearly so witty or laughable.

The element of surprise, then, while an essential ingredient of humor, can hardly be all there is to it. Not only is the incongruity theory, as we have seen, contradicted by the very material that confirms it, but we must sense that its aim is far too intellectual. It ignores the emotional, gut-level content of humor: the familiar, repeated expressions of lust, hostility, rivalry, or even the more delicate feelings of compassion and tenderness which put meat on the bones of comedy.

The degradation theory, in contrast, focuses directly on the emotional level. Hobbes's famous epithet, "The passion of laughter is nothing else but sudden glory arising from some sudden conception of some eminency in ourselves," Bain's assertion that "The occasion of the ludicrous is the degradation of some person or interest possessing dignity," and Leacock's picturesque notion, "Laughter begins as a primitive shout of triumph," all converge on the hypothesis that humor is essentially competitive, that the assertion of superiority and the putting down of others comprise the kernel of laughter.

How valid is this viewpoint? Let us see. The joke about the doctor and the dying men would seem to support it, for it clearly degrades the doctor by insinuating his incompetence and, in a general way, disparages the dignity of the medical profession. Besides that, satire, parody, and caricature all thrive on the exposure of some group's or person's weaknesses; insults, veiled or naked, are the common fare of many comics; and political humor, often savage, spotlights the cutting edge of wit so vividly that no one can deny it.

"I don't make jokes," Will Rogers once declared. "I just observe the government and report the facts."

Gibes like this strongly tempt us to agree that downgrading others and bolstering our self-esteem are indeed the essential motives behind laughter. But is it really so? If it is, then what do we say to those rare but wonderful times when we laugh at ourselves, when we admit and ridicule our own shortcomings? And what do we say to nonsense humor?

Q: What is purple, weighs ten tons, and is found in the sea?
A: Moby Plum.

Q: How can you tell if there's an elephant in your refrigerator?
A: You'll find his footprints in the cheesecake.

Whatever our age, we may smile at these quips; yet who in the world can they be construed to disparage? To claim that they are assertions of superiority is itself a joke. We may all admit to hostile impulses directed against our oppressors, against all those who are higher up in the social scale, against pompous people and coercive institutions, even against our friends and families. But there are few of us, I hope, who nurture deep resentments against whales, plums, elephants, cheesecake, or logic and language in general.

The degradation theory, like the incongruity theory, delineates an important component of humor: in the one case, an emotional component, in the other an intellectual-perceptual one. Incongruity, it may be said, applies most neatly to the form of the ludicrous but ignores or underestimates its content, while degradation applies directly to a large portion of its content but avoids or skirts its formal elements. Neither hypothesis is wide enough, however; neither encompasses the full range of the subject.

Neither, in addition, comes to terms with what is probably the most significant characteristic humor possesses: its ability to lift our spirits, to lighten our hearts, to inject vitality into a drab or burdensome mood. No theory can lay claim to a subject without grappling with its central qualities, and what is more central to humor than merriment? Let us not overlook the obvious: we all *like* to laugh. From infancy to old age, regardless of intellectual or social status, people in all groups and cultures enjoy a smile or a chuckle. Laughter, in short, is fun. It is gratifying in itself, no matter under what conditions it has been elicited. As such, it is part and parcel of our capacity for relaxation, ease, delight, for happiness in all its many hues. Any explanation of humor that professes to dig to its roots must keep this point in hand.

The liberation theory does precisely that. It elucidates the entire, varied range of things that make us laugh, omits neither intellectual, perceptual, nor emotional components, and—most important—makes convincing sense of the fact that wit and comedy are, above all, delightful.

What it claims, in essence, is that our sense of humor frees us from the constraints of conventionality, morality, reason, and other restrictive forces. So doing, it naturally makes us joyful, for any release of our vitality is bound to be pleasurable.

With regard to jokes and other forms of wit, it also provides a more comprehensive explanatory system than the other leading theories. Let us examine once again the story about the doctor and the dying patients. We have already recognized that it involves, in the punch line, a rendering of incongruity, and have also noted that it disparages the image of medical competence. We will do fuller justice to its impact, though, if we grasp it as a vehicle of liberation. The punch line, "My last wish is to see another doctor," is a freeing agent on at least three counts. First, in diverging from the path of conventional piety, it releases us from our bond of conformity, from our compulsion to act and speak as our society expects. Second, the Jewish patient's skepticism airs our common distrust of doctors, especially when our life is in their hands. And third, the ingenious proposal "to see another doctor" gives vent to our instinct for self-preservation, delighting us in its portrayal of a man who may be down but is not out—a posture we must all hope to emulate when our time comes. As a unit, then, the story liberates us from piety in the face of the eternal, from respectful appreciation of our superiors' ability, and from passive acceptance of our inevitable demise—no mean feat for a paltry joke!

The incongruity and degradation hypotheses easily fall into place as aspects of the liberation theory. Incongruity is simply the experience of liberation from expected images or thoughts, while disparagement of others is nothing more than the liberation of our aggressive drives.

Some objections, nevertheless, can be raised against our position. The first arises out of the fact that liberation from inhibiting conditions need not await the exercise of laughter. It is readily achieved without it. A man can dispel his inferiority feelings through successful, serious endeavor; he can shed his moral scruples by indulging in lustful adventures; he can rise out of mental mediocrity in the appreciation of great art. He can, in short, discard conventionality, rigidity, and all the rest without ever cracking a smile.

This being so, we must admit that while liberation may be a constant accompaniment to laughter, it is not identical with it. Agreed and agreed. We need exert no effort to rebut this line of reasoning, for it does not invalidate our argument. It forces us only to reclarify our aims. We have sought to establish only the kinship of laughter and liberation, not their interchangeability. Our primary goal, in fact, has been a practical one: to analyze our sense of humor in such a way that we might enable ourselves to develop it more fully. If that goal has been attained, then this study has hit its mark. Theoretical impeccability has been, for our purposes, a distinctly secondary consideration.

Another objection to our approach is somewhat more intricate. It applies most directly to the topic of laughter at unconventional behavior and it centers about the question whether such laughter proceeds from sympathetic identification with the comic object or from hostile disdain toward it.

We have asserted that laughter at unconventional behavior involves a vicarious release from the conventions that bind us, suggesting that our pleasure emanates out of a fancied freedom based on identification with the comic. Opponents of our viewpoint, however, argue that such laughter betrays a mood of self-righteousness, its pleasure being based on ridicule of those who don't know how to act as properly as we do.

The issue is debatable. When we laugh at the Marx Brothers making a shambles of propriety, I think it obvious that we experience a sense of release through identification with them, not a haughty feeling of superiority to them. When we laugh at a rival's clumsiness at a social gathering, however, I would not deny that our pleasure is rooted in a sense of superiority. There are many comic characters, I know full well, who elicit not our sympathy but our contempt. When a caricatured Jewish mother runs along a beach, screaming, "Help help! My son, the doctor, is drowning!" we enjoy the conceit of feeling, in comparison to her, unencumbered with stupid pride. Even this, however, is a kind of liberation—not from conventionality but from our feelings of inferiority.

The motive pattern underlying any specific instance of laughter varies with the characteristics of the stimulus and with the needs of the laugher himself. The liberation theory does not stand or fall, however, with the dominance of identification over denigration, for liberation as we have portrayed it includes the release of hostile feelings as part of the spectrum of disinhibition. One way or another, therefore, when we talk about laughter at unconventional behavior, or at any other form of ludicrous display for that matter, we are talking about the process of liberation. (Or, as some joker will inevitably observe, any way you cut it, it's still baloney.)

Having mentioned the main objections to our theoretical position, perhaps we can strengthen our convictions by recalling observations which support it. First, it is a well-established fact that both unusually restrictive situations like a classroom lecture or a church sermon and usually disinhibiting situations like a state of inebriation or a joyful celebration are conducive to an increase in humor. The remark or gesture that is only mildly funny in our everyday routine becomes hilarious when expressed beneath the teacher's stern glare or under the influence of a few martinis. Clearly, then, our general state of inhibition or disinhibition plays a significant role in our readiness to laugh. When highly uninhibited, we are emotionally and mentally so loose that the weakest stimulus is enough to set us off. When highly restrained, we become so needful of release, our spirits so desperately crave a moment's relaxation, that again the weakest stimulus will trigger our response.

Second, a fact of interest to any student of humor is the differential response that various types of jokes elicit. Notwithstanding the intelligence or excellence of the wit involved, those jests that produce the loudest laughter generally deal with tabooed subjects: in our culture mainly sexual promiscuity. The obvious implication is that the intensity of the suppressed impulses released by humor, even more than the skill of the humorist himself, determines the degree of enjoyment that occurs.

It remains to be said, of course, that despite this supporting evidence and all other arguments that might be marshaled to bolster our position, our approach to humor is not by any means the last word on the subject. Nor it is meant to be. Every theory or explanation, as a system of logic and language, is doomed to partial representation of a phenomenon like humor, for in essence the ludicrous spans the boundaries of reason and words as it emerges out of a deeper, prior realm of being.

Tonsils

*Any book that boasts an appendix deserves
a set of tonsils too. Our organs have their
sensitivities, after all, and ever since the
invention of the printing press they have
suffered and gurgled and slipped their discs as
the appendix, and only the appendix, has
been recognized and honored.*

---

*Now that I have taken up their cause,
however, and shown their need—indeed, their
demand—for equal representation, I expect to
see new texts being published complete with
kidneys, livers, and lungs.*